MODERN
MEDIUMSHIP

*A Complete (Woo-Woo-Free) Course to
Become a Successful Psychic Medium*

JOHAN POULSEN

JOHAN POULSEN

Printed Worldwide
First Printing 2022
First Edition 2022

Hardcover ISBN: 978-91-527-3818-4
e-book ISBN: 978-91-527-3819-1
Audiobook ISBN: 978-91-527-3820-7

To you, my clients and students over the years. Thanks to your spiritual interest and willingness to learn, you have given me the opportunity to keep doing the work I love. Thank you!

Table of Contents

Introduction

As I sat in the beige leather armchair waiting, I could hear my heart pounding. I had been preparing for almost two hours, trying to meditate and relax. I had lit a candle, topped up my water, and buffed the support pillow for my back. Everything was perfect, other than my heart-rate. The clock showed five minutes to ten, and I was just about to do a private reading for my first "real" client. I had done lots of readings before, in courses and workshops, and there had never been any problems. My journey as a developing medium had spanned over twelve years, and this situation had always been the end goal. But still, in that small room in the old town of Stockholm, Sweden, I could not get myself to relax. The thought of living up to clients' expectations made me tremble, and all I could think about was me, myself, and my performance. Just as it turned ten, there was a knock on the door. My client was here, and there was no turning back.

Welcome to the Journey

Welcome to this book and this course in Modern Mediumship! My name is Johan Poulsen. I'm a full-time medium from Stockholm, Sweden, and for the last thirteen years I have been working with private readings, groups, platform demonstrations, students, and TV. I'm thrilled you decided to read this book, and I'm looking forward to being your teacher on this journey. But first, I have to tell you that everything went fine with that first client! I got booked by two more clients the day after and by a couple more the day after that. It snowballed, and eventually, I found myself doing about five hundred private readings a year for a while. But I will tell you a little more about who I am soon. For now, let's focus on you.

If you are reading this, chances are you have been interested in mediumship for a long time. Most people who read these types of books, take courses, or attend workshops have usually had a lot of time to think about it before starting. Especially since mediumship is more than a hobby, it's like a feeling. For many people it's like a little spark, an inner knowing that grows over the years until it finally becomes too real to ignore. I suppose this may be the case for you. Or, maybe you haven't thought about it at all, but something about this book resonated with you when you stumbled across it. It's the same thing. You still have that inner spark, you just haven't thought about it. Either way, I've got good news for you—you are about to learn mediumship. And when I say "mediumship," I mean talking to people's loved ones in the spirit world.

There are many views and explanations connected to the word "mediumship." As you develop your skills and embark on this journey, you will meet many people who explain and teach this subject differently than I do, and that's okay. To be honest right from the start, the course I teach here is based on my experiences working as a medium over the years. I don't claim to be the superior expert on this subject because many mediums have been in this industry longer than I have. In this course, I'm offering you the knowledge, exercises, and techniques that have worked for me and produced excellent results for many of my students. So, I'm saying that if you follow this course and do the exercises, you will get results. No, I'm not here to sell you some new, complex belief system! Instead, I will give you the "toolbox of mediumship," and then it is your choice how you use it.

One important thing I need to be clear about from the beginning is my point of view regarding mediumship, how I see it, and how I work with it. I see mediumship as a sixth sense that every human being has and something we can all develop. It's not a special gift given to a few select people. Mediumship is like every other sense in the body. It's the same as seeing, hearing, feeling, etc., and is present from birth. When we see it like this, for what it really is, it becomes an easier concept to grasp.

Another thing that is very important in my work as a medium, especially so when working with students, is separating mediumship from what I call "drama." Listen carefully now. When I say drama (we will talk about this in detail later), I'm not saying this negatively or judgmentally. I'm saying this because it's a human condition, and you need to know what I mean in order to see it when it happens. Drama is that extra stuff, like a thick blanket on top of mediumship—it's theories, fears, and endless rituals. But it's okay if you want to use this stuff in your work as a medium. Whatever works for you and creates a loving atmosphere for your clients, do it! But whenever someone talks about the "scary stuff" of mediumship, that's the drama talking.

You see, mediumship is like a ball wrapped in velcro, and over hundreds of years everything from religion to all the different types of new age philosophies has gotten stuck to it. The concept of mediumship has become so big and theory-filled that it's sometimes hard to see that ball underneath the velcro. So, I'm here to show you that ball, the core of mediumship, to help you develop the actual senses that receive information from the spirit world. When you can do this, talk to the other side, and your clients confirm you are having a conversation with their loved ones in spirit, then you are free to put this skill into any context or terminology you wish. So once again, I'm not here to give you any new beliefs. I'm here to provide you with the skills to find your own truth.

My goal for you

My goal with this course is to give you not just an introduction, but a foundation. The platform you need to take your mediumship to the highest level possible. This course's information, techniques, and exercises are all you need to become a successful medium. Rather than trying to add as much as possible, I will do the opposite. I will peel away the excess so you can see that velcro ball, the core of mediumship.

Many years ago, a wise old medium gave me this advice: "If something is not working, go back to the basics." I have found this to be very true. Whenever there is a challenge in my work (and yes, there are challenges even when you work full time as a medium), I always go back to the basics. I peel away whatever new belief I have put into my mind and go back to the basics because it works.

So, in this course, I will give you the theory and techniques behind successful mediumship (that's left-brain work) and the exercises that will open up your senses (that's right-brain work). I will not only show you that mediumship doesn't have to be complicated, but further will teach you to be relaxed and confident as you develop and work. I will also give you an understanding of the trade and work of a medium, and most importantly, I will teach you how to get a strong connection to the spirit world. When this course is over, I want you to feel proud to call yourself a medium. All you need to do to get there is follow the steps and exercises in this book.

Who am I?

It's important that you feel comfortable throughout this course, and if you are going to let me teach you how to communicate with the spirit world, you probably want to know who I am. But, to avoid boring you with an "all about me" story, I will try to make it a teaching opportunity. So, here we go!

Something a little unique to mediumship is the fact that many of the people interested in it have never done anything about it. There are thousands of books, courses, and lectures, but most don't take advantage of them. So, why is that? One common reason is that they don't think they can do it. Or, they are just not interested in taking part. They may like to watch mediums work, but lack any desire to learn to do it themselves. Fair enough. But this takes me back to my main point. How can we feel such interest and pull towards something we haven't really explored or maybe don't know much about? We feel like this because the gift or skill of mediumship exists within all human beings, and the part of us that creates this interest is our intuition, trying to tell us that there is something within calling for our attention.

My journey started as a young boy in Sweden. I come from a very non-spiritual soccer family, and we spent most of our free time doing different sports. Then, when I was nine years old, I lost my mother to cancer. Being so young, I had a strange reaction to this experience—it presented itself as shame. I felt different because I didn't have a mother and was ashamed of this difference. I developed a powerful intuition to protect myself from any situation that would trigger this shame. I would read people and situations to avoid conversations that could lead to questions about my family, mother, or anything that would generate these feelings. I didn't know I was doing this; I didn't know I was reading people all the time. However it became a very effective tool for self-preservation. As I grew older, the shame disappeared, but the intuition remained. The spark was lit, and the interest and pull towards mediumship soon followed.

Like most young people, I didn't have time to think about mediumship or spiritual development. I didn't even know what it was. And it wasn't until my mid-teens that I actively started seeking information on the subject. I had a lot of existential questions, mostly connected to my mother, and despite being a little skeptical, I was drawn to the somewhat definite nature of mediumship. I decided if a medium could deliver a message from my mother about what I had in my pocket at her funeral all those years ago, then this was more than just woo-woo (and yes, this actually happened). So, I started to read and listen to meditations. Though, this was still in the early days of the internet when there was no Google, and you had to "dial up" the internet to get a connection. So, needless to say, most of my research came from books.

A couple of years went by, and suddenly all these courses and workshops popped up. I did everything from mediumship and healing to tarot and angel courses. I went to anything that was even slightly oriented towards mediumship. I started in Sweden but soon traveled to other parts of Europe to meet and hopefully learn from the mediums I had read about in all those books. I did one-day, weekend, summer, and full-length two-year diploma courses. I even did two long NLP coaching courses because I knew I would someday work with clients, and I probably needed to sort out my own "childhood luggage" before starting to help other people. And then finally, at thirty, I found myself in that beige leather armchair in the old town of Stockholm. Ready to work but very nervous.

Today, I'm forty-three and over the last thirteen years, I have worked with many clients—everything from private readings and stage demonstrations to house calls and students. I have an online course platform here in Sweden that, as of writing, has helped around 1300 students to develop their psychic and mediumistic skills. I've had the opportunity to spread my view of mediumship in interviews and magazines, and Warner Bros has kindly put my work in front of a TV audience in the show "Swedish Mediums." It's easy enough to see that the spark lit all those years ago is what led to the life I live today. I live in a house (some say a farm) on an island in southern Sweden together with my fiancée and our two children.

So, this is my story and how it all started for me. But a big part of it has nothing to do with mediumship. I was not a medium when I was nine years old; I was forced to develop my intuition, and today I understand how it all fits together. You see, intuition is the first step in mediumship. That gut feeling we sometimes have is the exact mechanism used in mediumship. We don't need to have lost a parent for this to get activated within us. Often (but not always), our intuition's trigger goes hand in hand with a strong emotional experience, and we have all been through something: bad relationships, heartbreak, a bully, illness, an accident, addictions, or a rough childhood. It could be something that happened when we were a child or an adult, age doesn't matter. All this stuff triggers intuition, and it's our body's way of protecting us from similar situations in future. Sometimes we listen to this intuition, and sometimes we don't.

But it's vital you understand that because of this intuition, no matter how strong or subtle it feels, we have already done more than half the work on our journey towards developing mediumship. And when I look back now and understand how it all works, I can confidently say that the information in this book would have saved me ten years of spiritual development had I known it earlier. So, as you start this journey, know that much of the groundwork has already been done for you. You don't need to change or become someone else to do this. Just follow the steps, be who you are, and your mediumship will follow.

Before We Start

Before getting into the meat and potatoes of this course, we need to be on the same page. Anyone who has had an interest in this for more than ten minutes knows that the world of mediumship and psychic abilities is filled with mixed and contradictory information. Some say one thing, some say another, and I believe we have more experts in this area than in any other. So let me be the first to say that I don't know everything, and I can't explain precisely how the universe works. But what I *do* know is based on personal experience, and my point of view has served me very well. Focusing on the actual core of mediumship (the velcro ball) and disregarding a lot of new-age stuff, I have been able to work in a relaxed and harmonious way for many years, helping lots of clients along the way. When you can describe a person in the spirit world and deliver a message to their loved one, the client in front of you, there's no reason to add a lecture about fifth-dimensional rainbows.

Common misconceptions

Before we start, I just want to go through three common misconceptions among students at the beginning of their development journey. Throughout this book, we will explore (and debunk) many other things connected to mediumship, but these are the most common things I hear from beginners.

1: The misconception that mediums are "special people" or were born with this "special gift." That's not true. I can tell you that all successful mediums have undergone some development training. They have trained to do this just as thousands of people do every year. A common question I get is, "Do you think I can do this? I've never had any spiritual or mediumistic experience." Yes, everybody can do this, even you!

2: This takes us to the second misconception, that mediumship is hard to learn. No, it's not. It's all connected to what we discussed earlier, your intuition. Your intuition is already active within you and has done half the work—the "senses" used in mediumship are already working for you. You just need to learn how to listen to them. They are the same senses that react when someone is lying to you, when you think of a person five seconds before they call you, or when you can sense something is amiss in a relationship. So, mediumship isn't as challenging to learn as many think.

I'm going to make a bold statement here: most students that come to me for a mediumship development session usually get pretty good and specific information after the first hour, even if they have never done it before. And that's not because I'm a unique and fantastic teacher; I know I don't need to teach people how to do it. It's already there, within them. What I do is point out where to focus. I show them how to distract the brain from everyday mental noise and focus on the body's senses. Within the context of mediumship, these senses are called "clairs," which you probably recognize from the word "clairvoyant." Once a student understands everything, development is usually pretty fast.

To emphasize, intuition comes first. We work with our intuition and develop our senses and clairs through "psychometry," which is the art of reading objects. When that's done, we enter the psychic energy field (we will explore this later). Psychic energy or readings means reading the people still alive, the energy in which we all live. When our psychic skills are all in place, and we know how our clairs work, we can then start connecting to the much subtler energy of the spirit world. And remember, the doors to the spirit world don't suddenly swing open. It's a very gentle and loving process in which you are always in control. The spirit world won't talk to you until you are ready to talk to them.

3: And finally, the third misconception is that it takes a long time to develop mediumship. No, it doesn't. Before my thirteen years as a working medium, you could say that I spent about twenty years in development because this intuitive process started when I was nine. So, like many other mediums, I could say that I've been doing this for thirty years. But the actual time I spent doing development exercises was much shorter, and those twenty years were mostly spent thinking, wondering, traveling, and searching for information. Mediumship and psychic development is something that continues our whole life, we are never finished or "done." But getting your abilities to a professional working level doesn't have to take long. Students on the online courses I work with today have access to all course materials for two years, though they are free to complete them at their own pace, and most of them graduate in six to eight months. So if you do your best and have the right intentions, I promise you this journey doesn't have to take long. And I will show you how to do it, every step of the way.

Course layout

This book and course is split into ten steps, with each including up to five different topics. Some steps are just information, while others also include exercises. Each exercise will include clear instructions explaining how it works and what you must do.

As I mentioned in the introduction, I have tried to peel all unnecessary information that could take us off-topic. Therefore, throughout this course, the focus will be on you and how you progress. If something seems unclear or questions pop up, keep going. The answers will come. Sometimes, we get a little impatient when we don't understand something. We want the answers IMMED-IATELY. But just keep going, and the pieces will fall into place. So, there are ten steps, after which you will find a bonus section to conclude. This section relates to your future as a medium, but there is no point in skipping ahead as the steps all build on each other. I also recommend that you use a good-quality notebook or journal during this course that will stand the test of time. Remember the advice I once got: "If something is not working, go back to the basics." This notebook or journal will be your "basics" that you can return to over and over whenever you need answers.

And just as a quick side note: if you already have prior mediumship experience and feel you need more advanced stuff and not basics, then stop. There is no advanced stuff. I'm saying this from a place of love. If you are reading this right now, this is the stuff you need. If you were a hundred percent confident in the "basics," you wouldn't be looking for courses or more "advanced stuff." No, at this point, you would be working and doing successful readings. The search for more advanced and complex answers is the same as drama. In step four of the course, I will talk about energy and the difference between "mental energy" (in the head) and what I call the "soul's energy" (in the heart) and how most challenges we face in mediumship (and in life) are connected to mental energy, our brain. And that's also where drama lives. Mediumship is something we do from the heart, the soul's energy, love, or whatever you want to call it. Even if the form of mediumship I teach in this book is called "mental mediumship," we still do it from the heart. There will be more on this in step four, but the "mental" aspect comes from the fact we translate the information in our minds; the head is thinking and the heart is feeling. In mediumship, we *feel* the interpretation of the information, then we *translate* it mentally. This will all be very clear before we finish.

Steps 1–10

In step one, we will discuss the difference between intuitive, psychic, and mediumistic work. In step two, we will talk about stillness, finding the place or state of mind where we can see, feel, or hear the information. In step three, we will look at getting started and go through the exercise sheet. Then, in step four, we will talk about energy, how to read it and work with it, and we will do some exercises. In step five, it's time to get a little more serious and talk about you, your emotional fitness, and how there is nothing to fear in mediumship; fear is drama. The spirit world can only work on a loving vibration. In step six, we will look at divination, which is reading cards, runes, colors, etc. We will also discuss the differences between divination and mediumship. The seventh step is devoted to connecting and working with spirit contact with related exercises. In step eight, we will discuss how to work with clients and mediumship ethics and morals. In step nine, we will prepare for your future as a medium and talk about working with groups and demonstrations of mediumship. And finally, in step ten, we will look at what happens after this course. After these ten steps, you will find the bonus section where I give you my best tips, tricks, and insights to help you in your future work as a medium.

So, that's the structure and content of the course. If it feels like I'm jumping ahead by mentioning something we haven't discussed, relax, and the answer will come as we move forward. One vital thing is, of course, the exercises. Mediumship is very much based on feelings, especially in the beginning. Much of the information comes through feelings, so we must know where and how to listen to them.

The information I'm giving you in this book will appeal to one side of your brain, and through the exercises, we will learn to use what we know and how to connect this information to the other side of the brain. The exercises are easy to do, and I would like you to approach them with a playful mindset. Have fun when you do the exercises. Mediumship is something joyful. Sometimes, when we work with clients, it can be sad and emotional, but we still do it from a place of love. That's the joy, the joy of spirit.

Clients and training partners

I know this may come as a shock, and this is usually one of the biggest hurdles, but you will need someone to be your client or training partner in most exercises. This can be anyone from a friend or relative to someone in an online community. So, yes, I would love for you to reach out and find other students, friends, or family with whom you can work and practice. You can be on different sides of the world and meet up through Skype. That works fine. The most critical thing in mediumship development is training. Everything you learn in theory must be anchored with practice. And I know from my own life and experiences that, in the beginning, some people want to make this journey in secret. We are unsure how others will react to our interests, and we don't have enough experience to feel confident being open with our mediumship. Trust me, I know the feeling. But the spirit world is intelligent energy. They understand us and what we are going through. They will answer by giving us information when we show them we are willing to be open and embrace our development. When *we* commit, *they* commit.

As you develop your mediumship, you will also grow as a person. Mediumship is about helping others—as you develop, you will feel this side of you getting stronger. When we learn new things in our life, things that we like, we also become more confident. We become more of who we truly are. And by opening up to new people, saying, "I'm a beginner, but I'm willing to learn," we not only grow as people, but we also give the mediumistic side of ourselves much more space to grow. Once we start, mediumship is something that develops continually, not only when we are doing exercises. Doing a course like this is like telling the spirt world that you want more of this, which they will give you, and so you get more of what you are interested in.

After a while, you will begin to pick up on, or just "know," things that you normally wouldn't. These are your senses getting sharper and starting to interpret the energy from your surroundings as information. For example thinking, "Oh, Susan is pregnant," or "Jonny's car had a flat tire this morning." This is all normal and will be clearer some days than others. If you are stressed and have a lot on your mind, the information can be a little weak—it's more accessible if you are calm and rested. Remember, there is nothing scary or wrong about this. It's normal. You have probably already picked up on information without realizing throughout your life. The difference now is that you will learn to see and feel yourself doing it, which is when this information becomes useful.

Important note

In the early stages of our development, we don't go around telling people everything we pick up on. This is important. If you pick up on something about another person, keep it to yourself. We will talk about more this later in the course, but one basic rule of thumb is we only work when we work, meaning we only give messages or information to people who have asked for it. Mediumship can be a little too strange for some people to understand or handle, so we don't want to force anyone into an uncomfortable situation. And it's also important to know that in the beginning, much of the information we get can be wrong. That's not because our connection or skills are weak, but because we haven't fully worked out how to interpret the spiritual language, feelings, or pictures we are getting. For example, for someone that sees information in pictures (that's called clairvoyance) it can be very symbolic. So a picture of an egg could literally be an egg, or it could symbolize anything from a pregnancy to a new job. Over time, we establish our spiritual language through exercises and feedback from the people we work with. This language will be unique, and other mediums may have a completely different meaning connected to that symbol. But until we can clearly understand our spiritual language, we must keep our mediumship within the walls of a training environment.

When I teach mediumship, I only have one rule. This is that it's one hundred percent okay to be wrong! Whether you are in the beginning stages of your development or have been working full time for twenty years, you will still sometimes misinterpret information. The sooner you take this rule to heart, the faster and more relaxed you will be in your development. All mediums get it wrong from time to time, even the ones you see on TV. We are all human beings, and when we interpret mediumistic or psychic energy through our body the human brain will sometimes jump in and get it wrong. A new job can be interpreted as a pregnancy. Even though clients are usually not talking when we do readings, they will tell you when you are wrong, I promise. That's why you must learn to be okay with it. And sometimes they will say you are wrong even if you are right, and in that situation, just be wrong. It's okay.

We don't do this work to convert non-believers; we do this to help people. So by being honest and admitting that we are wrong sometimes, or by telling a client that we're having a bad day and can't reach their loved ones on the other side, we are being professional. People know when we are connected, they feel it. They know who or what we are talking about and never question it. If we, for some reason, can't get a link to the spirit world on a particular day and are honest about it, then they won't question that either. What they *will* question is if they can sense we don't feel connected and we start claiming that we are right regardless.

So, stick to the course for now and only work with people that know you are in the development process. The day will come when you feel ready to open the doors to the public.

Step 1: What is Mediumship?

I hope the introduction gave you a clearer picture of the course and a good feeling for what's to come because it's time to jump into the actual course. We will start by answering the question, "what is mediumship?"

The word "mediumship" can probably be defined in a million different ways. My way has always been to simplify things to their core. So my definition goes like this: mediumship is communicating with someone's deceased loved ones in spirit. Years back, I spent some time in the English spiritualist tradition where they defined it as proof of life after death, which is also correct. It doesn't matter how it's explained. What's important is to note that the word "mediumship" is always associated with a "connection with the spirit world," the other side. This is something we will touch on soon to discuss the differences and why this is important.

Mediumship is very real and something we take seriously. But "seriously" doesn't need to mean boring, sad, or negative—rather the opposite. A reading or demonstration can be both funny and uplifting. I know some mediums who are excellent at balancing evidential mediumship and humor, a perfect mix between joy and tears. It's beautiful to see. So when I say we take it seriously, I mean we respect the spirit world in the same way we respect friends and family who are still with us. Going to a medium should be something uplifting, but also note that we don't just say stuff to make people feel happy. No! We present the information, the spiritual connection, in a kind and loving way, so that even when things get emotional or sad, the client still receives information in a caring and supportive way. You cannot control the information coming from the spirit world, but you can control how you pass it to your client. And remember, the way we speak to other people is always a reflection of ourselves and who we are.

For example, if your client had a grandmother that was always grumpy, the grandmother's spirit may come through and tell you, "I'm her grumpy grandmother," but the spirit is not grumpy on the other side. The grandmother's spirit is telling you this so your client can recognize who it is. At which point the client says, "Yes, absolutely, that's my grandmother. She was always grumpy." So, there you have it. Both a link to spirit, and a client who knows the person in question. But you don't have to be grumpy to relay this information to your client; you are still you. So if a spirit connection comes through and says, "I lived a very lonely life," they may communicate this by giving you a feeling of loneliness, but it's not your own feeling. It's communication. So don't sit there with your client feeling all lonely and sad. It has nothing to do with you. Give the information, and the feeling will disappear. The spirit world has no interest in stalking you or giving you bad feelings— you are just the channel, the telephone. They want to communicate with your client, their loved one, sitting in front of you. So "seriously" means doing the work lovingly and respectfully. And, of course, mediumship is not a party trick, so if we do it for the wrong reasons, it simply won't work. Your commitment to helping your client opens up the actual doors to the spirit world. When you do the best you can to be of service to the spirit world, they will do the best they can to help you get the information. Working like this is one of the most fantastic and rewarding ways of helping people. It feels incredible when you can help someone get a good connection.

It may sound like an effortless thing when I talk about mediumship. That's good, that's the way I want it to sound. And if you feel that maybe you should have studied this subject a little more before you did this course, no, you shouldn't have. You are in the right place. If you take away all the stuff you ever heard, the rituals and drama, you'll see that the core basics are not so complicated. It's a sixth sense, and you don't need to "go and get it"; it's already there. Of course, like anything else, we all have differing levels of talent at the beginning, but everybody, all mediums, have to do the same work in the end. Mediumship is not like building a pyramid brick by brick. Mediumship is like easing into a new season, like a warm spring after a long winter. You learn the "basics," i.e., the core, the "ball" in the center of mediumship, then this matures and grows by itself. All you need to do is nurture it through stillness (more on stillness soon).

What's the other side like?

A very good and frequent question I get is what the other side is like. What happens when we transition into the spirit world? This question is even bigger than the mediumship one, and you can probably get at least a million answers to it. But honestly, no one can tell you precisely what it's like. There are as many explanations as there are mediums, and these explanations are all based on individual experience and perceptions from our work. As you continue your journey as a medium, you will find your own interpretation. My answer to the question is that the soul is like a book with a hundred chapters, and one of those chapters is in your body right now, but the other ninety-nine are still on the other side. I call this the "soul book" and, when we die, the single chapter returns to it. Extending this theory further, we could say that our family, friends, and loved ones are like a library on the other side, and we are all constantly connected. When we do mediumship, we connect to the client's library. And for those who have questions about reincarnation, I say that if someone reincarnates, they send down another chapter of the book. That's why, in mediumship, relatives can always come through even if they have been gone for forty to fifty years. For me, the other side feels very vibrant and alive, and it might sound strange, but it sometimes feels like there is more there than here. It doesn't feel like we are going away; it feels like we are going home. But the time we have here, on earth, is very important. This is the time and place where our souls grow.

How do we know the spirit world is really there?

How do we know the spirit world is there? How can we know it's not just some psychic mind reading? Well, because the spirits will answer our questions. And I would like you to make a note in your journal that asking questions is one of the essential tools in spirit communication. So, silently in your head, ask them questions, ask them to clarify things, and ask them to give you something specific. If we don't ask questions, they may communicate in a more general way. For example; "I see a lady, and she looks old," which might be a hundred percent correct, but you want something more for that lady. So, ask her in your mind, "Please, give me something specific, something that connects you with my client." And the lady in spirit may say, "Your client has my first name," or "She wore my dress at her wedding." That's the importance of asking questions, and by doing this, you also understand how we know they are there. It feels like you are talking to someone you just can't see in the room.

I hope this has answered some of your questions about mediumship. And as I said, because of different mediums' experiences over hundreds of years, the word "mediumship" has become so big that we could easily do a separate book on this alone. But a book like that would have a more philosophical focus, and that's not what I want for you. I'd like this course to give you the knowledge and techniques you need to develop and work as a medium. The philosophy and your view on this subject will grow by itself over time. Even writing about this now is helpful for clarifying my own views and philosophy as it lets me put my own words to my beliefs. Similarly, as you continue your journey, you will answer so many of your own and others' questions that will help paint your picture of what mediumship is to you. Don't let anyone tell you what to believe. You'll figure it out by yourself.

Spirit guides

As an example of being influenced by other people's beliefs, I want to tell you a short story. If you have been interested in mediumship for a while, you have probably heard or read something about "spirit guides." These are not our relatives. This is a spirit on the other side that both helps us develop as humans and, if we are mediums, helps us in our work. You can find many explanations on how spirit guides work depending on the source of your information. And don't get me wrong, I'm not telling you what to believe. I'm simply shedding some light on a general question. Some say you get one spirit guide, some say three, and others say ten. Some talk about guides and angels as the same thing, and others clearly separate them.

At one point in my development journey, I thought I had a clear picture of my "team" on the other side. I went to England to study with a well-known medium I greatly admired and respected. When I asked about my spirit guides, this medium said, "Spirit guides. . . . That's a little 80s, isn't it?" I hope you get my point here. Many great mediums out there have their own unique picture of how it works, and even if they see or work with it differently, they all still get fantastic results. So my conclusion is that there is no single way to do this; find your way.

And as a side note, when I do readings, I never talk about guides or angels with my clients. I usually use the word "energy" when explaining things because it's easier to accept for someone who has little knowledge or is new to this. But for myself, in my work, I use one guide. If I work with students, it's different. I tell them what I am saying to you now. And by the way, don't let anyone tell you who your guide is. You will figure it out by yourself. If someone says, "your guide is a monk from Tibet," it may be correct, but if it's not, that picture will stand in your way of finding out who your real guide is. Give it time, and your guide will come and introduce themselves.

The three energies

In this section, we will talk about the three different energies: intuition, psychic, and mediumistic. I will explain the difference between these energies and why you need to know them. These three energies often get a little mixed up. You could say that these are three different types of "information" or various "tools" in your mediumistic toolbox. One is not better or fancier than the other; they are just different. And when we separate them, we can also see where the information comes from. This may sound complicated, but in effect, it's not.

Intuition

Let's make this into an example. Say it's your birthday, and on your way home, you suddenly feel that something is going on at your house. Even if it's all calm and quiet as you open the door, you know that you're walking into a surprise party here. And . . . surprise!! You were right. This would be an intuitive feeling, which is often just a hunch or gut feeling. It's usually connected to you and something you are about to experience. Also, parents, especially mothers, commonly have strong intuitive feelings connected to their kids. So, everyone has intuition, and even the most spiritually skeptical person can recognize this feeling.

Psychic abilities

Now, you are at this surprise party. Everyone has calmed down, and it's just a nice party. You stand in the kitchen talking to your sister, and suddenly you see a picture (in your head) of her and her husband changing the roof on a little cabin. So you ask her, "Oh, did you buy a little cabin?" to which she says, "How did you know that?!" That picture or piece of rather specific information would be "psychic information" you are picking up on from your sister's energy field. You are reading what we call psychic energy, and what some people refer to as the "aura." Even though "aura" is the correct term, you are interpreting the information from this aura using your psychic abilities, and that's how this information becomes "psychic information." This is not the spirit world, this is information stored in your sister's energy field. She has been thinking about this cabin so much lately that the energy of the whole thing has become very dominant in her aura. Thus, you could say that psychic energy, or a psychic reading, often deals with your client's life or life situation. During this course, many of the exercises will be connected to this type of energy and a lot of information will be psychic. Psychic energy is like "reading," and mediumship is like "listening." In psychic work, it feels as though you can zoom in on stuff and dig in deeper, while in mediumship, it feels like you need to be more patient, and let it come to you.

Mediumship

Moving on with the surprise party, let's say you are sitting on the couch talking to Steve at some point later in the evening. Steve is your friend's new boyfriend, and you have never met him. While you are talking, you suddenly feel as if a third person is present, sitting next to Steve. You experience a very affectionate feeling, like when you were young and visiting your grandfather. Suddenly you hear, see (in your mind), or feel like this person is talking to you and saying, "Tell Steve thanks for finishing the boat." And then you ask Steve (which you probably wouldn't do if he didn't know you were a medium, but let's say he was totally into this stuff), "Did you finish building your grandfather's boat after he passed away?" And yes, Steve finished the boat. So, this is an example of mediumship or mediumistic energy, and I hope these different examples make the three energies clearer.

Working with the three energies

In the future, you will work on all three levels in any given reading. Even if you don't know you are doing it, you will go back and forth between them. Holding an open link and connecting to the spirit world for extended periods takes a bit of training. You usually lose the link or connection several times in the beginning and have to go back and reconnect again. If I use myself as an example (and this goes for all mediums I have ever seen), and I'm doing a stage demonstration between one and two hours long, I know I will lose the "link" or connection to the spirit world several times. Either between the spirit contacts or in the middle of one. Usually, it's just a couple of seconds, and after a glass of water, I'm "linked up" again, but sometimes it takes a little longer. If this happens, I'll make a psychic connection to someone in the audience:

"Hi, did you lose your mother's neckless in a bucket of red paint?"

"Yes, I did!"

Okay. And then, building on the psychic energy, her mother comes in on a mediumistic link, and the demonstration continues. But the necklace was psychic energy I picked up from the audience. Now I just listen, feel, and see what the mother has to say and I'm back to mediumship and mediumistic energy again.

Summing up this example, you could say that the three energies represent three different abilities and levels of development. Once you have learned and mastered the last level, mediumship, you can access all the previous ones. But not the other way around. So, a medium can work on a mediumistic, psychic, or intuitive level but the psychic works on a psychic or intuitive level. And everybody is intuitive. It's not better to be a medium than a psychic. Many psychics do fantastic work and have really learned to focus and interpret the energy we live in. Psychic readings usually have more of a wow-factor, while mediumship has more of an emotional aspect. In countries like America and England I know they often separate the two terms, medium and psychic, but in many other countries (like Sweden), we only use the word medium.

So why is this important? Well, some clients don't want a mediumistic reading; they want to hear about their life, they want a psychic reading. Some people want both. If you get booked to do a group or a stage demonstration, they expect you to do mediumship, to work with mediumistic energy—the spirit world. If you are unclear about your services, you risk disappointing your clients. Even if you do fantastic work, your clients may be expecting something else. They wanted to connect to their husband on the other side, but they got an angelic card reading about their current workplace atmosphere. Or the opposite, they had questions about finding their true love, and you spent forty-five minutes talking about uncle George from Finland, whom they have never met. You see, there is nothing wrong with these two readings, but they don't fit your client's expectations. I personally don't believe in "I'm the medium. I decide what's important to you." No. Some clients say, "I'm not interested in the spirit world," and you must accept that. So it's always important to be clear about what we do and what energies we work with.

Babysteps

I started my business and company doing psychic readings. I named it "intuitively" and didn't use the word medium. I had a clear description of what I did and how I worked on my website. Then, when I was ready, I changed the name of my business to "Medium Johan" and edited the website to match my work as a medium. Many of my old clients and Facebook followers from "intuitively" went away, and after a while, I got new followers and clients who were more in line with my mediumship business. I still do a lot of psychic stuff in my work, but I always start every reading with at least one spirit link, so my client and I know I'm connected. And as far as possible, I let their loved ones in spirit give me the information before I go on to the psychic energy. If I switch energy, I tell them, "Your father says this," or "I'm picking this up from you." So, as you follow this course and do the exercises, you will be on your own path to "mediumship," and you will be able to work confidently with all three energies.

Different types of mediumships

As you go along on this journey, you will see and hear of the many different ways people work with mediumship, and it's good to have a basic picture of these different types.

Mental mediumship

What we are doing here, in this course, is called mental mediumship. We pick up information through our bodies and mediumistic senses and translate this information into words. Nothing happens in the room except for the medium speaking. As mediums, we may see, hear, feel, smell, etc., many different things when we connect to the spirit world, but in most readings, the client will never experience this themselves. Their experience will be based on the information we give them and their own related emotions. Mental mediumship is also the most common type of mediumship and is usually what you see in readings, stage demonstrations, and on TV. As mental mediums, we work with the three energies (intuitive, psychic, and mediumistic), but the experience for the client becomes one cohesive stream of information. In mental mediumship (or any type of mediumship), no dark clouds or ghosts are flying around the room. All that stuff is just drama. But, on several occasions, I have had the lights flickering as I begin a reading. No big deal, it's all just energy.

Trance mediumship

Trance mediumship has become hugely popular over the last couple of years. Originally, trance mediumship was based on "transfiguration," which is when a spirit shows its face over the face of the medium through a process called "ectoplasm." The client would see their relatives' faces, and the spirit can also speak, through the medium, in their voice. But, due to the long development process and experience required this is, unfortunately, very rare today. Nowadays, trance mediumship is something completely different. If you go to a trance demonstration you will most likely see a medium in a meditative state, with closed eyes, channeling information from a spirit or a guide. They often have a control person sitting next to them, taking care of them. In my experience of observing these demonstrations, the information often feels a little more philosophical and not as "evidential" as a mental mediumship demonstration.

Physical mediumship

Physical mediumship is when the spirit world manifests physical things through the medium. This is either stuff you can hold in your hand, audible voices, or things moving or happening in the room. A physical mediumship demonstration is usually conducted in a room with a small group, and all participants can see the things brought into physical form. These types of demonstrations are also very unusual these days. The interest in physical mediumship has not had the same growth as mental mediumship, and for many clients, the physical stuff still feels a bit too woo-woo.

And the list goes on . . .

Besides the examples above, there are also many specialized forms of mediumship, such as medical mediums, mediums who work with animals, and chakra mediums among others.

Walk before you can run

There is one important thing I need to mention when we talk about these different types of mediumship, and I'm sorry if I step on someone's toes here. . . . To do more specialized mediumship styles, like trance or physical, you first need to learn and master "normal" mental mediumship. These specialized disciplines are fantastic but take a lot of mediumistic experience to develop. You need to know and master the basics before moving on to the next step, and most mediums never go into these disciplines. So here is the "stepping on toes" part. I see and meet many people who have spent years in mediumship development, some much longer than I have. They have gone to courses and workshops half their lives and are still struggling with their mediumship. You see, there comes a time when you have to take the leap from student to working medium. This leap will bring up all the insecurities, fears, and confidence issues you have ever had. These are not "spiritual" problems but human "limiting belief" problems. And on that threshold, many talented mediums pull the brakes as they step out of their comfort zones. They listen to their fears and decide they will do trance mediumship instead. They permit themself to go back to "student mode," and suddenly, the natural flow of their development slows down. I call this "the trance trap," and I see it all the time. I'm not judging or being negative. I understand the psychology behind this. But I'm telling you, there will come a point after this course when you have to choose to step into your power and either become the medium I know you are, or jump on the next course.

Spiritual truth

You are probably starting to get a clearer sense of my view and philosophy on mediumship. I call this book a "woo-woo-free" course on mediumship for a reason. Over the years, I have had a lot of questions from students telling me about challenges they've experienced in their development. Most of these challenges have been connected to some trending new-age-based belief. There is nothing wrong with new-age beliefs, but they have nothing to do with mediumship. Mediumship is a technique that we develop, through which we gain the cooperation of the spirt world with our intentions of serving our clients. It doesn't matter what religion you identify with or which spiritual rituals you have incorporated into your life. Mediumship is separate—even the most hardcore skeptics can develop these senses.

So, I have said it repeatedly, and you probably get it by now. In this course, we are talking about the techniques and steps you need to take to develop your mediumship abilities. But see the "skill of mediumship" as a separate thing, a sixth sense. When you know how to do it and get the information, you can package this skill into any niche or context you like. Spirit, angels, dolphins, or unicorns, it doesn't matter. No one has a monopoly on spiritual truth. You follow what feels right to you, not what sounds right when other people say it. I have always been proud of working with teachers on both ends of the spectrum, mediums from both the spiritualist tradition and the (for me, more modern) angelic tradition. And all the mediums and teachers I met, regardless of the belief system they represented, were excellent and got fantastic results. That experience taught me that there is not one single way to work with mediumship. Their "techniques" were the same, but their works' context and niche differed.

The good opinion of others

Whatever spiritual niche or vocabulary you choose in your work, know this: the other side will always be a hundred percent loving, without exception. Anything else is drama. Your spirit friends will comfort and support you, never demanding or controlling you. If it works and you get information that resonates with your client, you are doing your job. Whatever rituals or routines you need to get in the right mode are up to you. Just be nice and ask the other side, "Please work with me today," and "Thank you for your help today." Follow what feels right to you and stay away from the opinions of others. Walk your own path, do the exercises in this course, and get to know your friends on the other side. If your intentions are good, and you work from your heart, than you can't get it wrong. There is no need to go up and down the mountain, around and around the chakras, and say everything three times just because someone says to.

But if you want to, and if it feels right and works for you, then do it! I'm not sending you blindfolded into a dark forest here, no. I'm giving you a bright light so you can see your new friends, and learn to know and work with them in a comfortabe and loving way.

Step 2: Turning Off the Noise

In this step, we will talk about stillness and turning off the noise of our everyday life. You may already be familiar with the concept of quieting the mind through meditation, yoga, or similar activities. And this is pretty much the same thing. Stillness is stillness; there is no special spiritual stillness, it is all spiritual.

If you have prior experience with any form of relaxation or stillness exercises, you will know that results can fluctuate. Some days it's more accessible, and on others it's impossible to quiet the mind. Being a medium doesn't automatically make it easier to do this. We are still humans with daily tasks, responsibilities, and challenges, and we need to learn where we fall on the "stillness spectrum." We need to be able to recognize whether our minds are silent enough to receive information. And, sometimes, they're not. That's just life. It's hard to pour more water into a full glass.

Stillness is one of the essential keys in mediumship—the ability to switch focus from your own life to someone else's and listen with your senses without putting new information into an ongoing thought process. I just like the expression, "leave your bags at the door," because that's what this is all about. Before doing a reading, we are usually occupied with our own lives. During the reading, we switch that off and instead use our senses to receive information. Then, after the reading, we go back to our own lives again. In mediumship, it's common to use the terms "opening up" and "closing down," and you could say that "stillness" is half of this process. First, you still your mind, then you "open up," which basically means you raise your vibration to match the spirit world. Then to "close down," you just return to "yourself," and you pick up your "bags at the door" again.

Stillness

The first step to stillness is creating a daily routine, and in the first exercise in this course we will do just that. Your daily routine or stillness exercise is something you will learn and hopefully do every day, or at least four to five times a week. Over time, you will probably create your version of this exercise—most mediums do. Other than being an essential step in your mediumship development, this daily stillness routine will also positively impact your everyday life as you learn to relax more.

In stillness, we listen to our bodies and our emotions. We learn to recognize the mental noise and the thought processes connected to us and our own lives. The more we do these exercises, the easier and faster we can shift to the right energy or state of mind to do mediumistic work. After a while, the body and the brain recognize what we are doing, which will take us to the right place faster. But, if a lot is happening in our lives at one moment, it can take longer to find stillness. Some days it takes thirty minutes, while others it takes only one. So, when doing this, always give yourself enough time and make sure you are stress-free.

In the beginning, I want you to do the first exercise daily for thirty days. If you can't do it every day, that's okay. It will just take a little longer to get used to it. For the first week, this exercise will be just like relaxation, and it will probably come with a pleasant and calm feeling. If you get emotional or feel other feelings, that's okay, too. It's just old stuff coming to the surface. Observe it and let it go. As you continue this course and learn to know and recognize psychic and mediumistic information, this same exercise will begin to feel different. And that's the whole point. Your energy will shift, and you will become more aware of what's happening inside you.

For example, imagine holding a glass jar filled with blue and white marbles. The white marbles are "you," your memories and thoughts, and the blue marbles are information from the spirit world. The more you do the exercise and learn to raise your energy frequency, the easier it will become to separate the marbles. So in the future when you do a reading, it is the blue marbles, the spirit information, you will interpret to your client. The white marbles will always be there, but you will know the difference between your thoughts and the spirit information you receive. Your brain will always try to sneak some white marbles into your stillness and readings. In a reading, you may get twenty pieces of information right and then suddenly one piece of information wrong. And instead of going, "No, I know I'm right," you will know to recognize that a piece of your own thoughts, a white marble, sneaked in there. No problem.

I have tried to make this process as simple as possible, and if you stick to it, it will get you in the right frequency to do mediumship. All I ask you to do in the upcoming exercise is to simply sit still and listen to relaxing or meditative music for twenty minutes, nothing else. Of course, like anything in the world of mediumship, there are a thousand variations to this exercise. Some mediums work with the chakras (energy points in the body), others with angels, and others go up and down a mountain. It doesn't matter. If it works, it works. I'm saying this because when someone tells you to do it one way or another, you will understand that it's okay to do it your own way. If this routine becomes a complicated ritual, too much of the human brain is involved, and the blue marbles disappear.

When you sit in stillness, you don't have to do anything or expect anything to happen. You just sit there, listen, and relax. Don't try to communicate with the spirit world or wish for something to happen. Just sit. When you sit with the intention of raising your frequency and developing mediumship, they will know it on the other side. They will help you strengthen the link or connection you need in your future work. And just as you are slowly learning to know and recognize their world, they are learning about yours, who you are, and how they can work with you in the best way possible.

The process of stillness and opening up is connected to our inner bodies and souls. Mediumship is communicated from souls in heaven, through your soul, and then to the soul of your client. Or, as one of my mentors said, *from* spirit, *through* spirit, *to* spirit. So when we work as mediums or on our development, it's on the soul level. And when we are finished, we go back to our everyday lives. We are still people in a physical world with bills to pay and dishes to do, so we don't stay and live in the stillness. We go there to develop, to work, and then come back. If you have heard of "grounding yourself," this is it— stepping back into your regular life. And by the way, living in a monastery or ashram won't make you a better medium. And having a glass of wine or smoking a cigarette won't make you a worse one, either.

Spiritual focus

Before jumping into the stillness exercise, we need to talk about spiritual focus and how to point this in the right direction or place for spirit contact. By shifting our frequency through the stillness exercise, we can access the subtle energies that contain information. In the beginning, this will mostly be our clients' energy and psychic information, but the goal is to learn to recognize the even more subtle energy of the spirit world. Our body will need to get used to this, so just observe what's happening the first couple of times you do the exercise. After a while, you will learn how to stay in that right place and hold your focus there for an extended period, and then the information and communication can begin.

For example, when someone has a small baby, they tend to pause the TV, sit still, and listen for sounds from the baby. They don't focus on that sound all the time, but they have that radar or connection with the child. They switch focus from the TV to the child as soon as something is detected. And, of course, that child is super important to the parents, so that link to the child in the other room works instinctively. Even if you have no prior experience as a parent, from the second that child is born, you have this built-in skill that tells you about the child even when you are focused on other things. And many mothers will tell you that even when the child is eighteen years old and traveling on the other side of the world, that link will still tell them if something is wrong.

And just like in this example, the mediumistic senses are also built in from the beginning. The difference is that we haven't put any focus on it. But when we develop mediumship, it becomes like our child. We become aware of very subtle things coming into our minds. After a while, we just know stuff. But before that happens, before we get to a place of clear information, there is a short training period where almost nothing makes sense. As you start doing the stillness exercise the spirit world will begin working with you. But just like starting a new job, it takes a while to get used to everything.

Development phases

Before you practice the stillness exercise, I want to go through what to expect. I want to be clear about what's essential to your development and what's not. I usually say that mediumship development is eighty-five percent personal development because before we get clear enough to see, feel, or hear the spirit world, we typically need to see, feel, and hear the inner part of ourselves. Often, we need to clean out some of the stuff that we haven't paid attention to, that we have hidden under everyday mental noise.

First phase

This exercise can make people emotional the first time, and that's okay. Some people cry while others burst into laughter, you probably know your personality type. This is not a strange "spirit world thing," this is connected to you. These emotional experiences come long before you reach the place of the spirit world. Like a new job, in the first week you get your desk ready, learn the routines, and get all the keys and codes you need; this is the same thing. In the first week of the stillness exercise, you basically learn how it works. And in that process, your normal busy mind can offer resistance. That's okay, just keep going.

Second phase

The next phase of this is usually much calmer and is usually the first phase of their experience for people that have previously undergone stillness exercises or have spent time in personal development. They have already dealt with the emotional part. So, in this phase, the stillness exercise usually becomes an inner visual journey, like seeing a movie or traveling around the world or cosmos. It's also common to see a lot of spiritual symbols, colors, and have meetings with everyone from monks and native Indians to loved ones that have passed away. All this is nice and feels meaningful and spiritually significant, but it's not. Your brain will still fill up the stillness with "white marbles." But that's okay, this is all part of the process.

Remember what I told you in the introduction: I intend to peel away any unnecessary stuff and teach you this honestly and naturally. So I'm going to get a little honest here. This phase that I've just explained to you, the friendly, symbolic, going-on-a-journey-phase, is one many developing mediums will never get past. They like it too much, and the pictures and serene feelings connected with this are sometimes too nice to let go of. There is so much spiritual symbolism here that it feels like it must be the spirit world, but it's not. It's the brain. A reading connected to this stage of development will probably take the client to a fantastic temple filled with glimmering gemstones and the gift of a golden key or something like that. It's harmless, but it's not mediumship.

In contrast to this phase, a real mediumistic connection is a little boring. You see, it's a different experience. It has nothing to do with you and your inner world. You are just letting the information pass through you. And, of course, mediumship is not boring. It's nice, but more of an honorable experience.

Third phase

After the fantastic pictures, journeys, and meetings in the last phase, everything now slows down. Nothing seems to happen. Compared to the previous phase, it may feel as though you have gone backwards and lost your skills, but you haven't. You have entered the first "real" phase of mediumship, where things start to happen. And now, in this phase, your journal or notebook will play an important role. Now, when everything is quiet, you can finally hear, see, and feel the new stuff coming in—stuff you know is not yours.

You are still just observing what's happening, not putting any meaning or interpretation on your experience. You are looking for subtle physical feelings such as tingling in your body, something tickling your neck, or, as is very common, cobwebs over your face. There could be thirty different things coming and going, and I would like you to write these down in your journal. Over time, you will see a pattern. Some subtle feelings will come and go, but others, maybe only one, will return every time. This is called a "calling card" or a "recognition sign." The "calling card" is the sign from your guide, whether you know who your guide is or not (logically, you won't know who your guide is if they just started calling on you). So the calling card is a sign from your guide saying:

"I'm here, you're here, let's work together." This is where the exciting, real mediumship journey starts.

Fourth phase

Through stillness, you are now on the right frequency. And, by doing the exercise repeatedly, you will have pierced the mental noise and gotten your focus in the right place. Your guide is sending you the calling card, and you are now what we call "open to the spirit world." This is where your actual journey of mediumship starts. Everything I have discussed and every question you have had so far will fall into place. At this point, you are experiencing what we have been talking about, and you will see how my words were just pointers in comparison to the experience itself. In this phase, you will also understand how I can say that mediumship is not hard, because at this stage your guide will step in like a mentor from the other side and will begin to help you.

As with any new friend, you need to spend time together to learn to know each other. And there's no need to do anything new for this either, you do it through the stillness exercise. You go back to this place every day. You get the calling card from your guide, and you just sit and feel each other. Learn who this guide is, how they feel. Depending on how busy your life is on any given day, your mind may throw in a lot of white marbles, so don't grab the first Tibetan Monk or Amazon Warrior that comes along. Be patient, let your guide introduce themself over time, and don't let your mind post a complete picture from the beginning.

Getting ready

Now we are getting ready for the actual stillness exercise. And once again, I want to remind you about what I said earlier, "the answers will always be in the basics." This is the basics. If you, at any stage, in a week, month, or ten years from now, are having problems connecting to the spirit world, the answer is probably somewhere here. Your focus is perhaps not in the right place. In that case, start again and reconnect to make sure your guide is there. Without the spirit world, you cannot do mediumship.

And just a quick remark. We previously discussed "opening up" and "closing down," and in the stillness exercise, we do both. We do a simple visualization where we go "up" and end the visualization by going "down." As I mentioned earlier, the door to the spirit world doesn't suddenly swing open. It's a delicate process, and you must actively stretch your energy to get there. The second you stop trying, your energy falls back to normal again, like closing down. Most mediums, including myself, just say, "I'm done for today. Thank you, spirit, for working with me," and everything is then closed down. This is important.

You also can't get stuck in "open mode," and have spirits flying uncontrollably in and out of your life. No, it's not how it works. All that stuff is drama and is usually told by people who need attention or an excuse for the challenges they are facing in life. The other side, the spirit world, are the souls of yours and your client's loved ones. They communicate using the only energy that is powerful enough: love. They may have been grumpy and mean during their time on earth, but that stuff doesn't continue into the spirit world. All the problems and bad behaviors we humans have live in our brains, and we bury the brain when we die. The energy we connect with on the other side is the soul—the wise and loving part of that human, free from the challenges and behaviors of the mind.

Exercise 1 | Stillness

Now it's time to dive into the first exercise. The goal here is to learn how to quiet the mind so we can find the right place for mediumship and connect with our guide. In the introduction, I mentioned some different views and explanations regarding spirit guides, and what I'm teaching you here is how that works for me and my students. In the future, your way of looking at and explaining this process may differ from how I'm teaching you here, and that's perfectly okay. But for now, just follow my lead.

What I want you to do is find some relaxing and meditative music. Something that resonates with and calms you. If you already have some favorite music, you can use that. If not, just find something online or on Spotify. Don't get hung up on finding the "right mediumship music." Anything that gets you to relax works.

Make sure you set aside about twenty minutes to do this exercise quietly and calmly without being disturbed. You usually get the best results if you do this in the morning or when you are not too tired. If you fall asleep, get disturbed, or need to stop the exercise to attend to something important, it's okay. You can just go back and do it over again later.

First half

So, here are the instructions. Learn and remember these by heart. Sit comfortably in a chair or on a couch. Turn on the music, take a few deep breaths and just relax. Breathe in and out in any way you want to, and feel how your body relaxes. After a few minutes, visualize yourself being lifted from the chair or couch, slowly starting to levitate up towards the ceiling. When you reach the ceiling, you effortlessly levitate right through it and continue outside. Visualize your surroundings as you continue levitating upwards and see how everything gets smaller and smaller beneath you. You see your house getting smaller, your town getting smaller, your country getting smaller, and the whole Earth getting smaller. After a while, you find yourself in the vastness of space. Stay there and just relax. As you sit comfortably in this space, visualize a white light in front of you. Slowly levitate into this light and continue sitting there. Don't expect anything special to happen; just relax and observe. Let this part of the visualization take ten to fifteen minutes. Don't use an alarm clock; just go by feel.

Okay, now we have done the first half of the stillness exercise. This next part is important. When we do this exercise daily, by ourselves, to develop our senses and strengthen our connection to our guide, we must do both the first and second half together in one go. After doing the first part and visiting the light, we must then go back down using the second half.

However, when we practice, for example, readings with a training partner in future, we separate these two halves. So in upcoming exercises, you will do the first half of this stillness exercise to "open up," but you will then follow it up with whatever course exercise you are doing at the moment (e.g., a psychic reading). When you are finished with your exercise, you will then "close down" using the second half of this stillness exercise. The stillness exercise is a tool we use both to develop our higher frequency and to prepare for readings. There will be no precise moment when the first half stops and the second half starts. Just follow what feels right.

Second half

The second half of the stillness exercise is the same, only backward. After spending a couple of minutes in the light, you just say thank you and levitate out of there. Slowly and fully relaxed, you levitate down towards the Earth again. You can see the Earth getting bigger, your country getting bigger, your town getting bigger, and your house. Continue levitating slowly down, through the roof, until you land softly on your chair or couch. Take a deep breath, open your eyes, and continue your day.

After doing this exercise and visualization a few times, you will know it by heart. It's not very complicated. Don't get hung up on doing it "exactly the right way." We are talking about feelings and senses here. Just go with it. Do the visualization in a way that feels right to you. There is no wrong way. It's also up to you how long you want to spend in the light in the middle of this exercise, but five to ten minutes is enough. Aim to do this every day for a month minimum, and remember, don't expect anything to happen. The key word is "relax." By relaxing into this exercise, you are not only developing your mediumship, but you are also doing something very beneficial to your body. You are learning to relax.

This exercise will run parallel with the rest of the course, and new exercises will soon come up.

Moving forward, it may feel like we are doing a lot of things simultaneously, but that's okay. If you want to master the stillness part first and continue the course later, you can do whatever feels right. I recommend you do this exercise every day while continuing the course simultaneously. When we come to the part of the course where we start doing readings and related exercises, you should always do the stillness exercise first. You will use this first half to open up before any other exercises, then use the second half to close down when you are finished.

Step 3: First Steps

Now it's time to talk about the first steps in mediumship development. And yes, you could say that the stillness exercise was the first step. But I'm talking about the first steps you take once you have learned to "open up." These are not all active physical steps, they are more like experience steps. Your job is to get to the right place and get the calling card. Then, the rest is to follow the journey as your guide works with you. No matter how far you come in the stillness exercise, I will explain the development process from a position of being connected to the guide and open to the spirit world. If you feel you are not there yet, no problem. Just follow this course and when you reach the right place, you will already be equipped with all the information you need for the process to go smoothly.

Intention and trust

The first thing to know and learn once you start opening up to the spirit world is the importance of "intention" and "trust." Even if you are a very spiritual person and believe that the spirit world is waiting for you with every bone of your body, your mind will continue throwing "white marbles" into the process. These marbles will express themselves as doubt. This is very normal. "Am I really experiencing this, or am I just making it up?" This is something you have to learn to put aside. These forms of doubt will always be there, jumping in and making you question yourself from time to time. Our rational mind has a hard time handling stuff like this, going against the logic of our left brain—that's just part of mediumship. But the more you do it, and the more you help people and connect them to their loved ones in spirit, the easier it will become for the logical side of our brain to accept it.

Intention and trust are essential. For many people, "intention" is just a word, but in mediumship, it's everything. Sitting in front of a client or a large audience, you never know how good your connection will be or if you will get any information. So, you put your trust in the spirit world. If you open up and go in intending to do the best you can, then you will be fine. The intention to help someone is a thousand times stronger than the wish to perform well.

Trust is just trust, and the more you do mediumship, the more you feel that it's not just you doing it. You will feel a part of something bigger; you will feel the other side working with you, and you will trust them to help you. But first, you have to show up with intention and trust from the beginning, even when it seems like there is no one there on the other side. Intention and trust are the seeds of mediumship, and you must keep on watering these seeds regardless of whether you can see them growing yet. Once they begin to grow, they grow fast.

Patience

One thing that is also of vital importance is patience. Your guide and the spirit world will show up if you let them. But you cannot force it. If you try to, you will leave your heart and go to your brain where you will close down and start analyzing what's not working. Don't do that. Keep on watering the seeds—the spirit world will come.

Soon there are going to be more exercises in this course. And at first glance, they may feel a little too advanced. You may think, "But how am I going to do a reading when I'm not sure if I'm in the right place yet and don't know who my guide is?" You see, this is the intention and trust part.

You intend to do your best and trust that they will help you; then you just do it. Will you get it wrong? Yes! Will you feel like you can't do it? Yes! Will you be patient and continue doing these exercises, knowing that great things are happening for you behind the scenes? Yes. . . .

It's a common human condition to want to be really good at something before doing it, especially before doing it in front of other people. But mediumship doesn't work that way. You can't wait until you are perfect; you never will be. Mediumship is like life, we change and develop all the time. The day we reach perfection as mediums or human beings will be our last. So please don't wait. Go for it, and things will fall into place.

Doing readings

I want to talk about readings and working with others because that's what mediumship is all about. And not long from now, I will ask you to step out of your comfort zone and start connecting to friends and other people who share your interest in mediumship.

The stillness exercise will be your way of opening up before any exercises or readings. But I also want you to create a little "start-up routine" to do before the actual stillness exercise. The audio track is essential, but before you listen, I want you to calm yourself a little more. Take some time before you do the stillness exercise. Light a candle, put on some music, dim the lights and say a prayer if that's something you like. All of this is very beneficial and helps you get deeper into stillness. It also sets the intention. It doesn't have to be complicated, and you don't need any advanced rituals, just a quiet moment to tell yourself and the spirit world that you're preparing to do your work as a medium. Personally, I always take at least an hour before I see my first client of the day. And during that hour, I spend around ten minutes in the "opening up" process. But by taking time, slowing down, and setting my intention for the day, I feel I'm already halfway there once I start to open up. Sometimes I get my calling card before I even start, which means my start-up routine has already put me in the right frequency. Over time, your intention will do much of the work in getting you to the right place for mediumship.

Now, you are calm, in the right place, and have your client in front of you. It's time to listen. The information will be very subtle and probably won't come as you think it will. On the other side, your guide or spirit is pure energy, pure soul. They have no body, mouth, or vocal chords to speak with. So, to compensate for this, the spirit world will use different ways to communicate with you. Through the exercises, they will adapt and find the best way for you to receive information. In the beginning, everything will get mixed up before you find your way of communicating.

Clairs

The spirit world communicates with you through something called your "clairs." Clair is originally a French word meaning "clear"; it has become the go-to word when talking about mediumistic senses. A clair represents a specific mediumistic sense, and you have probably heard this used in words like "clairvoyance," which means "clear-seeing." So, all mediums have clairs, and one or two of them will likely be more dominant for you over others. The dominant clair will be the one that gives you the best and most clear information. For example, if the information you are receiving is along the lines of an old, happy but stubborn woman, or a feeling of someone having moved to a new house, then your dominant clair is clairsentience, "clear-feeling."

I'll go over the different clairs and tell you what to expect when it comes to communicating through these. Something that is the same for all the clairs is the speed of the information. It comes instantly. If you, for instance, get a "name" in your mind as you shake the hand of an arriving client, you can be sure that name will be important to your client as you start the reading. But sometimes the information comes so fast that we miss it. That's because we are usually more relaxed the moment before we start the reading, not expecting anything, which is also when it's easier for the information to pass through.

Clairsentience

Clairsentience means "clear-feeling." In my experience of working one-to-one with students, this is the most common clair. Information received through clairsentience is basically the spirit world talking to you through feelings. It's not waves of uncontrolled emotion, not at all—it's specific. If a father comes through for his daughter, you could start to feel like an older man.

I'm going to stop here and tell you something important: it's just a feeling—it's not you. Your body only has room for one soul, and that's *your* soul. No spirit can or wants to get in there. You don't get possessed, and no random "dark spirit" will take advantage of you because you are a beginner. All that is, you guessed it, drama. The spirits coming through are your clients' loved ones from the other side, and what the spirits do here is called "over-shadowing." They make their energy present and available for you to feel who they are. You tell your client what you are feeling, and the second you give the information, the feeling changes to tell you something new. For example, you may feel as though you have a "quiet but happy old man," and, upon relaying this information, you suddenly get a subtle stinging feeling in your chest area, sensing that this man had problems with his heart. And so the communication goes on. If it's a father coming through for his daughter, you will most likely also feel that father-daughter bond between them. Then that feeling develops, and the spirit gives you information about their relationship. All you are doing is listening, paying attention to subtle sensations in your body, and passing on this information to your client.

Over time, when you have felt a certain feeling many times, the information in a reading may start moving much quicker. If you have been to a stage demonstration, or séans as we call them in Sweden, you may have seen the medium pacing back and forth on the stage, the information bursting out. Not all mediums do this, but many do. Or, if you ever get the opportunity to see one of my TV episodes, I sit down, and my arms go like a windmill in a storm. I don't think about it; I just go with it. Some people like it, some don't. It's just the way I work. But all of this pacing back and forth or moving the arms are signs of the medium trying to keep up with the fast information flow from the spirit world. A typical sign of a medium with a weak connection to the spirit world is when they stop and think for long periods. If the link is there, the information comes fast.

Before we move on to the next "clair," I want to address a common question. "Are you communicating directly with the spirits of your client's relatives, or are you communicating with the spirits through your guide?" My answer is you are communicating directly with the spirits. After you have opened up, it feels like your guide steps to the side and stands there supporting you through the reading.

Clairvoyance

The next clair is clairvoyance, meaning "clear-seeing," and this can differ from medium to medium. But you can be sure that you will not see an HD-quality color movie in your head. It would be great, but it doesn't happen. It's more like seeing a photograph at the bottom of the sea when snorkeling. You see it for a fraction of a second at the right angle with the right light, and then it's gone. The picture can be very exact, it can be symbolic, and sometimes a reference from your own life. For example, you could see a red bike, which could mean a specific red bike, or the size of the bike may be pointing to the age of the spirit. It could even be your old bike which symbolizes freedom to you. It may sound a bit complicated when I explain it like this, but you will learn to know what the pictures mean over time. You will develop your own "visual language" with the spirit world, and they will know what pictures to show you. So, if you don't understand a picture, you can use your clairsentience and try to "feel" it. Clairvoyance can also be something subjective in the mind or objective, as in something you see in front of you in the room. Most likely, though, and especially initially, you will see these as pictures in your mind. And, besides, objective pictures in front of you in the room are still subjective. They are still in your mind, and your client can't see what you see.

Clairaudience

Clairaudience means "clear-hearing." This is when the spirit world uses sounds and words (subjectively in your mind) to communicate. It's the same thing here; they are not tuning in to your ears and giving you a forty-five-minute phone conversation. Like pictures, words and names pop very fast into your mind. "Uncle," "James," "lungs," etc. Mediums with clairaudience as their most dominant clair are usually very aware of this because they essentially "hear stuff." When you hear the information, it becomes very obvious to you as a medium. If you are not very clairaudient (like me), and it's just sporadic words and names here and there, you will be better off focusing on another, stronger clair.

Claircognizance

The fourth clair I want to cover is claircognizance, meaning "clear-knowing." The experience of claircognizant information is "to know without knowing how you know," you just know. The more you practice and do mediumship, the more you will feel like you get this type of claircognizant information. That's because you know what all the feelings and pictures mean, so you interpret the information so fast you don't think about it, it feels like you just "know." I have heard other mediums talking about how they seem to get more claircognizant over time and don't focus on a specific clair anymore. And I agree with that. As your body gets increasingly used to interpreting the information, you stop thinking about *how* you do it and just *do it*.

Other clairs

There are also a couple of other clairs like clear-smelling, clear-tasting, etc. If you happen to be one of the few mediums that receive information through smell or taste, then go with it; these clairs work by the same rules as the rest of the clairs. Smell it, taste it, and give the information to your client.

How to use your clairs

It's good to know that these clairs work the same way in intuitive, psychic, or mediumistic work. So even if you are getting more of a psychic connection than a mediumistic one at the beginning of your development, you are still going to work and develop your clairs. As long as you do it the best way you can, with an open mind, a playful attitude, and the right intention, your clairs will develop. At first, the information may seem wrong to your client, but that's because you don't yet know what your clairs are saying. Just keep going, and it will fall into place. Go with the first thing that comes: a feeling, picture, sound, or knowing. Never assume anything about your client. A guy dressed in rags can be the wealthiest man alive, and vice versa. The information comes fast, and if you feel you are searching for it, you are back in your mind. Just relax, let it go, and let the information come to you.

Allow yourself to be a student intending to learn. Be okay with being wrong initially and trust that your development is in full motion on the other side. Approach every exercise and client with a relaxed mind and know that whatever happens, you are learning to understand your clairs. You are learning the language of the spirit world—someday, not far from now, everything will fall into place.

The exercise sheet

Now it's time to introduce the exercise sheet you will use throughout this course. At first glance, this may look a little overwhelming. But I promise you that this sheet, and the structure that comes with it, is what you need to get your mediumship abilities in place. Everything we talk about on this course is something you have to translate into experience. Everything you need to get the logical side of your brain on-board with the process is here, but we need to take all this information, drop it down into the body, and begin experiencing this subtle inner world of information. You could say that the exercise sheet forces you to let go of logic and enter the world of your senses. When all the exercises are finished and the sheet is complete, you will have gained enough experience to tell the differences between "you" and "spirit information," and the difference between "thoughts" and "communication." And then, you can start helping your clients for real.

So, the exercise sheet is a way to log your progress throughout the course. Each time you do the stillness exercise, or one of the others, you just check them off on the sheet. And yes, I know, for some people, this sheet with all these exercises may create a feeling of "What? How in the world does he expect me to do these exercises? I've never done anything like this before!" I get it, and that's okay. It's like getting your driver's license. It doesn't matter how much theory you study, you inevitably need to get behind the wheel before anything can happen. And this may sound a bit strange, but even if you do this whole course and all the exercises and you never get one piece of information right, all you get are "no's" and "wrongs," you are still taking huge steps towards your future as a medium. The challenge, in the beginning, is not to get it right but to be okay with being wrong—its about a willingness to learn, even if it's not making sense. To stand up for what you believe in, say to yourself, "I'm a medium, I just need to continue the work." And the pieces will fall into place.

I remember walking into venues with fifty or more people that had all paid the organizer to come and see me, and until the second I started working, I had to be okay with whatever happened. It's not about us. As mediums, we are committed to being the link between the spirit world and their loved one, the client in front of you. They will use the opportunity to communicate if only we are humble enough and move our own brains out of the way. Today, I know that when I step up and put myself out there, I create the opportunity for mediumship, and it works. It will work for you, too, but you have to get behind the wheel to make things happen. If you finish the course and this book before the exercise sheet, that's okay. You can always go back and use the course steps to get answers and clarity. The more exercises you do and the more experienced you get, the clearer the steps in this book will become, and they may even start making sense to you in a different way.

Earlier, we talked about reaching out to other people and using them as clients when training, and this is an important thing. As you open up to the world and learn to know new people, you also grow your confidence. And this confidence will be a very positive boost to your mediumship. Your test clients can be anyone, such as friends and family that you feel are interested in the subject of mediumship. You can reach out to a local spiritual circle or start your own. The important thing is that you keep moving forward. If you find a local spiritual circle and they do this development process in a slightly different way or using a few different exercises, it's absolutely okay. The important thing is that something is happening and you are moving forward. All the exercises can be done over Skype, telephone, or in person. It stimulates the "clairs" in different ways when you use different types of communication. I personally don't do much phone work because I like to see my client, but I know I can get a good connection when I'm on the phone, and that's because I use less of my human senses (like my eyes) in this situation, and so it's easier to tap into the clairs.

On the next page, you will find the exercise sheet. After every exercise, you just need to check the box and move on. If you don't want to write directly in this book, you can just copy it to a separate document. This sheet contains all the exercises in this course.

Modern Mediumship – Exercise Sheet

Step 2 | Exercise 1 | Expanding in Stillness | 30 days x 20 minutes

Step 4 | Exercise 2 | Psychometry | 3 x 20 minutes

Step 4 | Exercise 3 | Psychic Reading | 3 x 20 minutes

Step 6 | Exercise 4 | Divination | 4 x 20 minutes

Step 6 | Exercise 5 | Stretched Psychic Reading | 5 x 30 minutes

Step 7 | Exercise 6 | Mediumship | 5 x 30 minutes

Step 4: Everything Is Energy

We are now on the fourth step of the course. You have seen the exercise sheet and hopfully have a better picture of what we are about to do. In this step, we will talk about energy and how the concept of it can help you answer many questions throughout your development journey.

So, energy is energy, and it has both a spiritual and scientific explanation. All the different explanations point in the same direction in the big scheme of things. Not long from now, someone will find a scientific explanation for mediumship. This explanation will be focused on photons, particles of light, and stuff like that and will probably not feel very spiritual. But, it's all the same thing. You don't need to focus on the scientific *explanation*—focus to the spiritual *information*. As long as your clients recognize who you are talking about, you are doing your job as a medium. So, let the scientists do theirs.

In mediumship, all forms of energy are neutral. There is no high and low, good or bad, light or dark energy. It's just energy. And this may come as a shock, but it's the truth. Many people on their spiritual path like to use the concept of energy as something good or bad. This reflects our mental drama, and we fool ourselves into believing that the other side is this world of light and dark pulling back and forth. But the spirit world is the pure energy of the heart, soul, and love. There is nothing on the other side trying to fool people, this idea is created here, in the minds of the living. And good proof of this is that people who are not interested in mediumship or spirituality don't usually have a problem with the concept of light or dark energy. They would logically have the most problems if it were true, but they don't. Because the problem isn't on the other side, it's in people's minds.

So all energies are neutral, the only real good or bad thing about energy is our reaction to it. Suppose you are doing a reading and the spirit contact talks about their life as having been very destructive or negative, or perhaps talks of a life filled with addictions or illnesses. In this case, they may send you these feelings to interpret through your clairs. These feelings will be very subtle and may represent a negative memory from their past life. But if you act as if these feelings represent the current moment and make them your own, then a reading can suddenly feel quite tough. Some inexperienced mediums hold on to these feelings because they trigger something within them, something that has nothing to do with mediumship or spirituality. A feeling received through a clair has touched an old psychological scar that scares them. Instead of observing, understanding, and taking the opportunity to grow past this scar, they blame evil spirits and dark energy. I suppose I don't need to underline the drama in this behavior. . . .

The same is true when it comes to positive and loving feelings, which is a much more common experience when doing a reading. When a loved one in spirit comes through, they send a lot of love through you to pass on to your client. Usually, we are not used to such an overwhelming feeling of love, and it's normal for many developing mediums to get very emotional, especially if the client gets emotional, too. This is a nice and positive reaction to love, but as you get more experienced, you will learn not to get involved with what's happening. You usually do a better job when calm and detached from what's coming through. Feel it, deliver it to your client, and let it go.

So everything is energy, and energy is everywhere. The spirit world is not "up there" or somewhere in a distant cosmos. The spirit world is here, all around us, all the time, and so is the energy of every person you meet and every place you visit. This is how mediums can "read" different things: pictures, cards, houses, people, spirits, and crystal balls. It's all an infinite bubble of energy around us. We are also made up of atoms and energy, and that's how we can read the energy of others. We don't read it like a book, we "blend" with it. Knowing how our personal energy feels, we leave that at the door and look for something else. That something, that other energy, will never replace our energy because our soul never leaves our body. When it does, our time in this life is up. By this, I mean that we temporarily and consciously let our bodies (our clairs) feel the energy around us. All human bodies do this all the time. It's a matter of self-preservation. We all read the environment, but as mediums, we do this on purpose. By developing our clairs and cultivating our stillness, we can choose to switch our focus and put it on anyone or anything: a necklace, a person, or a Scottish castle, and, of course, the spirit world. It's important that when you see the concept of energy like this, you also see that once you have mastered your clairs and mediumistic language, one thing is not more challenging than the other.

I will give you an example: I once did a house call, a group reading for a lovely family. I worked for about an hour connecting them to their loved ones in spirit, and then I asked them if they had questions. I like animals, but I have never had any pets, so I'd never felt this type of connection previously. This family, however, had an immense love for their dogs, and I had one beside me the whole reading. Unsurprisingly, the first question was related to a dog that had passed away and whether I could connect with it. I said, "I don't know, I can try," and it worked perfectly fine. The dog told me everything about an injury, old memories, and all the stuff the owners had kept in a box in the closet. They were super happy and emotional, and I was pleasantly surprised. But afterward, as I was driving home, it all made sense. They loved this dog as a family member, and by using my clairs and shifting my focus as I always do, this love came through the same way as any spirit on the other side would. Since then, I have had many experiences with pets, and some mediums specialize in this and only work with animal connections.

The point of this story is the same: energy is energy. Whoever or whatever you read, it's done the same way. And later in this course, we will talk about divination and the different physical tools you can use, but always remember what we discussed here. Any tools, cards, or crystal balls are only used to distract your logical brain, to help you leave yourself at the door. But the actual reading will consist of you reading energy and nothing else. The magic is not in the cards or any other tool—the magic is in yourself connecting to energy.

I hope this gives you a more detailed picture of what we do as mediums when we connect. Once you have developed and know your clairs, the only obstacle to what you can read will be your limiting beliefs. The way around this is simply to try. If someone asks, just try. It's okay if it doesn't work, keep trying, and it will work out.

Aura, chakras, and reading the future

Moving on, we will talk about aura, chakras, and reading the future. And guess what? It's all about energy. First, we need to separate these things into two groups, the traditional spiritual concept and their actual energetic properties in mediumship. For me to teach you everything about auras or chakras would take a very long time. There are thousands of books written on this, and you may already have prior knowledge. In the context of this course, it is necessary to talk about how you will experience and work with these auras and chakras and how you will feel when you work with a client and tap into their energy. I'm trying to keep the core, the velcro ball, as clean as possible here, so I'm not going to dive too deep into these areas. I'm focusing on the mediumistic part. As you develop your skills, there will be a natural urge to learn more, and over time, you may read up on these subjects. But at this point, there is a risk that this could steer us a bit off track and would involve too much mental gymnastics. So, I'm going to talk about it a little more generally, focusing on the experience you will have as a medium.

Aura

The "aura" or the "auric field" is an energy field that surrounds a person's body. It's often explained in different layers and colors. For someone quite interested in an aura's color, it's not too hard to learn to see them with your own eyes. It takes only a bit of practice. It's all about learning to shift the focus of your eyes, soften your gaze in the right way, and then see it. Learning to see the aura is not like riding a bike. If you don't keep doing it every day, you may find you can't quite reach the right focus or "gaze," and the colors won't be as clear. I also find that the actual colors of the aura can shift quickly, which is why I'm not a big fan of determining the quality of someone's life based on the colors of the aura. It changes depending on a person's state of mind. So it can be one color before a reading, different colors during the reading, and new colors after it. The only time I actively look for the colors of an aura is when I'm listening to a spiritual teacher or any person speaking about mediumship or spiritual matters. I look at the top of their heads to see the "light" or "glow" which is usually present when someone is connected to their higher self or the spirit world.

The aura is used in the same way as when working with all types of energy. You automatically expand your aura when you "open up" or "tune in" to do a reading. You make your personal energy bubble bigger so that you can use your clairs to blend your energy with the client's energy. The client's aura (energy bubble) mixes with your aura, and just like the white and blue marble metaphor, you separate what information is yours and what belongs to your client, and you do this by observing your clairs. So basically, we could say that as soon as you open the door for a new client, you will start feeling or reading that client. When you are finished and close down for the day, you tighten your energy bubble around you. Your senses will stop reading, and you won't receive any more information from your clairs.

Just as a side note, people who often describe a feeling of being energetically drained by other people are usually walking around with a bit too big of an energy bubble (aura). No, this is not caused by "bad energy" or "being born with mediumistic super powers"! It is instead commonly linked to curiosity as a personality trait. People who are very curious by nature tend to be drawn to other people's life situations. They focus on another person and, in the same instance, start to blend with their energy. Their intention may be kind and caring, but they still get sucked up in drama and situations that have nothing to do with them, and therefore, can't do anything about it. They start to live and experience someone else's problems, which drains their energy. It's not bad spirits or dark energy—their curiosity unknowingly compels them to interact with other people's auras. The solution to this type of experience is to tighten your energy bubble to stop blending with other people's energy. You do this by grounding yourself in your own life, which is what we do in the second part of the stillness exercise.

The aura is not only used in mediumship. Everything from healers, coaches, therapists, and salespeople also use this. That's how someone gets good at something. They read their client or their customer. Of course, they rarely know or talk about this, and this is often just explained as having good intuition. But by blending with the energy of their clients or customers, they get a feeling for what's necessary in the moment and can then act accordingly.

So the important thing for you to know is that this is happening all the time. The actual colors or layers of the aura are only necessary if you are interested in this subject. You can still work with auras in your mediumship, even if you don't see them with your eyes. It's good to understand that sometimes a client may tighten their bubble when they are very nervous or skeptical towards you or the reading. It may feel like they are pulling their aura in, stopping you from getting a grip on their energy or the information.

That's okay. In situations like this, I usually stop the reading and say, "Sorry, I'm not getting the connection I was hoping for." I always blame this on myself and never blame the client. I ask them to come back later, and when they do, they are usually more relaxed and the reading goes well.

Chakras

Chakras or the "chakra system" are different energy points in the body, and you have probably seen this shown through a picture of a body with different colored dots. Chakra is a Sanskrit word meaning "wheel," with each chakra point being an energy wheel rotating in the body. We usually talk about seven chakras, but there are many more if you study this in-depth. So you could say the aura is the energy field outside the body, and the chakras are the energy fields within the body. I know this is a general explanation, and I'm only lightly touching on this subject here. Some people spend a whole lifetime studying it. I'm simply keeping to the core of mediumship by not going too far down this road. The important thing is that you have heard about these subjects, auras and chakras, because they will pop up from time to time during your development journey. Many healers talk about the aura, and many mediums meditate to go up and down the chakras, opening them up. But we do the stillness exercise, which, at its core, is based on the same thing.

When do you encounter or use the chakras in your work as a medium? Well, normally, you don't. But you can study the chakra system and find out what the different chakras mean and what each color stands for. Then you can use this as a tool and clairvoyantly see these colors or clairsentiently feel the chakras in your client's body. For example, the "throat chakra" is connected to communication, speaking up or telling the truth. So, if you are working with the chakras as a tool, you will feel it in your own throat when a client has difficulty, for example, communicating the truth in their life. If you find this fascinating, you can study this in-depth and simply make it your tool. You can consciously focus your energy on the client's chakras and use your clairs to read them. There are some mediums called "medical mediums." These mediums focus on a client's health and are usually very good at reading the chakras. During the first years of my development journey, I studied much within the English spiritualist tradition, and I don't think we ever talked about the chakras. I had to learn that later, so you can still be a medium without in-depth knowledge of the chakras.

Reading the future

Let's talk about reading the future. This is one of the most common questions in readings and is also connected to energy, just like everything else. Usually, when you do a reading, you don't let your client ask questions from the beginning. You make a small introduction explaining how you work and start the reading. If a reading is forty-five to fifty minutes long, there will generally be a natural breathing point at thirty minutes. You have connected to their loved ones in spirit, giving the client their messages, and now both you and the client know you have a good connection. At this point, you can open up the reading, and the client can ask their questions. The most common type of question is about the client's future.

So, this is an important part. When you look at the client's past, you see and feel the actual lived-in history. The energy of what has happened in the past will not change. Then, if you look at the present moment, that energy normally also feels clear and solid. But when you look at the future, the energy is constantly moving; the future is not predetermined or fixed. The meaning of the future is for us as human beings to mold, create, and grow. We create our own futures and are a hundred percent responsible for our lives. The whole meaning of our evolution is to face and overcome any limitations or obstacles in our life and move towards what we feel we want for ourselves, our family, or our children. We live this life and face challenges for a reason—to grow as humans. But some clients don't like to hear this. If clients feel they don't have the willpower or courage to make the necessary changes in their lives, they want you to tell them that everything will work out. Don't fall into that trap. Don't give promises of gold, exotic adventures, and perfect relationships. If you do, you take the responsibility away from the client, and they could end up sitting on the couch waiting for it. I hope I'm clear here.

Looking into a client's future is a very psychic thing. Combined with the mediumistic part of the reading, you will usually also receive help from the other side. A mother in spirit could tell you to look at her daughters relationships, so you will then psychically tune in to that area. When looking at the future, you will pick up a "potential outcome". You see or feel where they, i.e., their energy, is heading. The future is like a tiny seed in the "now," and as a medium you see in which direction it grows. If the client changes their life, the energy or direction of the future will change with it. So, when you talk about the future, the client will know and resonate with what you are saying in the same way they did when you spoke of their loved ones in spirit. They will recognize the future you are talking about, which is how it becomes powerful. For instance, if you pick up on a new job, they have already had this thought in the "now"; that's the "seed." So you are basically confirming what they already know and highlighting stuff that may stand in their way. For example, "I see you have filled several applications for new jobs, but you never send them in because you're not sure if you're qualified enough for the type of job you want," this is the seed in the now. "But I also see you working for a much smaller company than you do now, and it feels like you are enjoying it," this is the energy of the potential future. You may see them working beside an old friend, and upon telling them this they may reply, "Yes, my friend runs a small family business and has offered me a job. I want it, but I don't know if I'm good enough, and I don't want to disappoint her."

As mediums, we don't make decisions for our clients. Their lives are their responsibility. Some clients have very low momentum in their lives, not much is happening, and the energy of the future will look exactly like the "now." It's not the medium's job to change this. When talking about this, always be clear about the "creating your own future" part. If there are no changes on the horizon for the client, go back and look at the now. Why is the client's life standing still?

And remember, with this course, you are on your way to becoming a medium, not a fortune-teller. Your focus should always be to connect your clients with their loved ones in spirit, and the psychic part of the reading should be a nice, pleasant bonus. If you work like this, you will always have a lot of new clients. People will recommend you to their friends, and you will be able to adjust to any situation. If you take the fortune-telling path in your work, you will only work with around five or ten people repeatedly, and they will expect you to make all their life decisions for them; that's not professional. More psychic work will be involved at the beginning of your career and during your first readings, which is understandable. But it will help if you always strive to get as much mediumistic information as possible into a reading because that's where you can help your clients and positively impact their lives.

Psychometry

It is now time to talk about "psychometry," in which you will recognize the same energy concepts we have already talked about. By now, you have a better picture of how we read different types of energy. We open up and focus on an area of energy—the energy of the spirit world or the aura of our client. Then we use our clairs to interpret the information through feelings, sounds, or mental pictures. It all works the same for psychometry, and you'll soon be doing a related exercise in this course.

So psychometry is when we read an object. It can be anything: a necklace, a watch, a scarf, a picture, etc. And we use this object to make a faster or stronger connection to the person or spirit we are reading. This works just as well for connecting to a loved one in spirit as it does for your client—these are the two options for psychometry. It is only a tool to get a stronger connection and is only used to get that connection with the spirit world or your client. If someone brings you a stolen necklace from their ex-husband's new wife, you shouldn't read it. I hope you understand what I mean. Psychometry is not used to delve into an outsider's personal life to enhance a client's mental drama. The object you read is simply used to get a good connection, and when that is done, you can put the object down and continue your reading as usual. Personally, I always wait before letting my client give me a picture or an object. I always try to get the connection with no help or tools first. If I feel it's not strong enough, I will try connecting through psychometry. I often don't need the object or picture they brought with them, but I ask for it at the end of the reading to see if it can give me some extra information. If the client brought something to the reading, it's probably very important to them, so it's nice to ask for it at the end, even if you don't need it. They like that. If it's a picture, you get the rare chance to see the person you already connected with during the reading.

How to do it

Hold the object or picture in your hand. If it's a picture, don't get too involved in the actual image. Instead, try to feel it more than look. The same goes for a piece of jewelry or something else. Hold it in your hand, focus on your clairs, and start working with the first thing that comes up. The actual information usually has nothing to do with the item you are holding in your hand. You are not telling the story of the object. You are telling the story of the person or owner of the object, the spirit contact. Once the connection is made, put the object down.

Psychometry is an excellent tool for developing mediumship. It's an easy process. You can do it on your own, in your own time, and it's a perfect way to learn and strengthen your clairs. Clothing tags, those little fabric labels on your clothes that tell you what temperature you should wash them at, are very useful in psychometric training. You can ask a friend to collect and send you a couple of these clothing tags from different people, each in a sealed envelope with no text. Then you can tune in, hold the envelope (never open it), observe your clairs, and write everything down. Then you send the still-closed envelope back to your friend, or the owner, alongside your notes and ask them for feedback. The owner of the clothing tag should be someone you don't know, so if you are doing this course with a friend, you can help each other out. The owner of the clothing tag also has to be aware and okay with you doing this. If you explain the exercise and what you will do, getting feedback on your notes will be no problem. Everyone likes a free reading.

Another part of psychometry is reading houses or places. It's essentially the same thing, just a much bigger object. If you, for instance, do a group reading at someone's house, it's not unusual to pick something up from the house. An important note here is that I'm not talking about haunted houses or picking something unwanted up. That's mental drama. For example, "this house used to be half its size" or "this castle was once burned to the ground." And of course, you can read the energy of the people living there.

You can get a spirit contact if the current owners are related to the previous deceased owners.

But this, like anything else, will be a connection of love. Don't buy into everything you see on TV.

Exercise 2 | Psychometry

This is the second exercise in this course. The first one was the stillness exercise, and I hope you have been doing it because it will help you now. So, this is the first "reading type" exercise we will do, and we will use this exercise to learn to know and recognize our different clairs. We will also determine which of our clairs is the most dominant: feelings, pictures, or sounds. As you can see on the exercise sheet, I want you to do this exercise three times for twenty minutes a piece. If you have someone that can give you more than three objects, perfect. You can do it as much as you want, but ensure a minimum of three times.

A huge part of mediumship development is confidence, standing up for who you are, and believing in yourself. A big part of this is also reaching out to other people, telling them what you are doing and asking if they want to help you with an object or a clothing tag. It doesn't matter if you reach out to a friend or a colleague. Of course, it helps if the people you reach out to are a little interested in this stuff or at least willing to participate. Don't force anyone into this exercise if they don't want to.

Another important thing to note is that this exercise is a psychic exercise, and you only want things from people still alive. You need to be clear about this and explain that this is a training exercise. There are no guarantees you will get any information, and the object owner needs to know this. We try to do all our exercises in a fun, loving, and playful atmosphere, so it's essential that everybody involved feels the same way.

Before you start

Before starting this exercise, you need to do the stillness exercise, but only the first half. As you know by now, the visualization of the stillness exercise goes from "sitting," going up to "space," and then "back down." Before the psychometry exercise, I want you to do this first part, going up into space until you are "resting in the light." Then you will do the psychometry exercises and the second part of the stillness exercise to finsh up. This may sound a little complicated initially, but it's easy logic. We raise our frequency, do the exercise, then go back down. We are not really going up and down—we are just changing our frequency through relaxation and teaching the body to go into work mode. In the future, you will know where on the scale or where between the "chair and space" you are, and that will determine how much preparation time you need before doing a reading. I talked about this earlier, sometimes it takes a minute, and other times it takes thirty. So, you are learning to know and feel where your frequency is. After doing this a couple of times, you will easily feel it.

Reading the object

After doing the first part of the stillness exercise, you take the object in your hand. Maybe it's a clothing tag in a sealed envelope or something else. The sealed envelope is necessary so you don't get any preconceived ideas. It's easier to listen and feel your clairs if you don't know what's in the envelope. And, of course, never borrow someone's expensive jewelry. If you lose a clothing tag, they can live with it, but not a diamond. So this object should be from a person who is still alive. Maybe a friend of a friend, but you should not know who the owner of the object is. You need to collect all the envelopes (a minimum of three) and ask your clients to either mark the envelope with a number or put their address inside. That way, when the exercise is finished, you can figure out who the owner is by asking what number they put or by opening the envelope and reading their name. But during the exercise, you should remain unaware.

Then, you hold the envelope and start going through your body and scanning your clairs. What do you feel when you hold the object? Listen to your feelings and write anything that comes up. Sometimes it's easier to record your reading on your phone or a dictaphone and then transcribe it later. When you have gone through your body looking for feelings, you go to the next clair. Do you see any pictures in your mind? Do you hear anything? Words, or names? Or do you just know stuff about this object? Write it down.

End the exercise

After twenty minutes, you can stop the exercise. Put everything aside and do the second part of the stillness exercise, from space to the chair again. Then, when that's finished, return the object with your notes to the owner and ask them for feedback. Make sure you have agreed beforehand on how and what is to be returned to the owner. If a friend helped you with the object, you could return it through them. If it's a clothing tag and the owner doesn't need it, you can send your notes through email. But always give the owner a couple of days to get back to you with their feedback—don't ask for it immediately. If you give them a few days, your notes will become clearer to them with time.

That's the whole psychometry exercise, and you will do this at least three times throughout this course. If you feel you can't find anyone to help you with this, that no one wants to participate in your exercise, then ask yourself why. Likely, you are not feeling confident enough to ask for help, and you need to build some more courage. This is both part of the exercise and the course—part of being a medium. People will come to you when they know you are on this path. But before that, you need to take the first step.

When I started my journey, I had no one. No spiritual friends and I didn't know any mediums. I couldn't find any events, fairs, or anything connected to mediumship. I thought I was the only one in the world interested in this, and I was a bit scared and unconfident and thought that people would think I was weird. But I reached out, took the first step, did a couple of workshops, and started connecting with people. Before I knew it, there were more events, fairs, demonstrations, courses, mediums, and new friends than I could ever wish for. For some, this will be easier, and for others, it will take a bit more courage to get the ball rolling. So, contact someone today or tomorrow and try to get these three items for your three psychometry exercises. Parallel to this, I hope you are doing the stillness exercise a couple of times a week. Just as a reminder, when you do the stillness exercise as part your daily routine, you do the whole thing, up and down. But when you do the stillness exercise connected to this or any other exercise, do the first half, then the exercise, then the second half.

Exercise 3 | Psychic Reading

So far, we have covered a lot of theory in this course, so I want to go through the next exercise right away. You will feel and understand the theory better once you start working and doing these exercises. So, we have gone through the psychometry exercise, and will now dive straight into "psychic readings." I know it may feel like we are moving fast, and it may seem like the different exercises are piling up, but don't worry. When we start doing these different exercises, the flow of this course will naturally slow down a little—first you need to find people and objects for your psychometry, and you are hopefully doing the stillness exercise frequently, and now we move to the next exercise.

To make it a little easier, you can do it like this. Suppose you haven't started or finished the psychometry exercise. In which case, you can still read through and complete this psychic reading exercise, and can and present it alongside the psychometry exercise. You can ask the training client for a clothing tag for the first exercise, then say, "After reading this object for you, are you interested in getting a psychic reading from me?" Two birds with one stone. If you don't know the person well, doing both exercises with the same person is okay. Any unclear information you picked up during the psychometry exercise may become much clearer once you get a chance to read the actual person.

After reading through this exercise, you could probably take a short break from the course and focus on getting the two last exercises done. But make sure to come back again. If the exercises take too long (say, more than a week), then go back to the course. If you ever feel stuck or alone on this journey, go back and keep reading this book. The important thing is not to lose momentum and to always keep moving forward. If you can't find the time to do these exercises, just read the whole book and go back and do the exercises later.

Before you start

As always, start by doing the first half of the stillness exercise. You will soon notice that the foundation of this exercise is much the same as the psychometry exercise. And like I said in the section about energy, all readings are simply you reading energy, so just like reading a clothing tag, you are now reading a person. You can do this live, on Skype, or over the phone.

Reading your client

After a quick introduction between you and the client, ask the person you're reading to relax and be quiet. Then start listening to your clairs. Just relax. What do you feel, see, hear, or just know? Whatever is coming through first, give that information to your client. Don't interpret or try to make sense of it. Just say it, and if your client feels the urge to comment or talk, ask them to please hold the feedback until after the reading. The reading will be twenty minutes long, and if absolutely no information comes, you will sit there quietly for twenty minutes. No matter how awkward or wrong you may feel, don't stop the reading before your time is up.

The difference between reading an object and reading a person is not the reading part or the information part; the clairs work the same way. The difference is that you have an actual person in front of you, expecting you to give them a psychic reading. And as human beings, we usually don't like to be bad at things. So, in this situation, we tend to tweak and twist the information to make it fit into what we think is suitable for that person based on who we think they are. Don't do that. It's very normal for developing mediums to try to be a little too nice when doing a reading, and that's because they are not confident in their skills yet. To get around this, ensure your client is aware you are a mediumship student undergoing training. Tell them you can't guarantee they will get any information. And most importantly, don't take the whole thing too seriously. In the beginning, when you ask someone if you can read them, do so lovingly and playfully, and set the bar for expectation low. This way, the client will be relaxed, you will be relaxed, and soon you will feel, "Oh my god, I don't know how I did it, but it worked!" And that's because when you are relaxed, you can get out of your own way. And then you will see results.

Some small reminders

Just a few small reminders from earlier sections. You do the first half of the stillness exercise, do the reading, and when you are all done and have said goodbye to your client, you close down by doing the second half of the stillness exercise. The first and second halves of the stillness exercise are something you do by yourself, before and after the reading. Your client will not be in front of you, waiting for you to open up or close down.

Always ask for feedback after the reading, but ask them to mail it to you. You could ask them to take notes during a psychic reading and then email you later. We also discussed a little startup routine, calming down, and maybe lighting a candle before going into the stillness exercise. I want you to start combining these before every exercise. I also want you to work on a simple little introduction that you can use before you read a client, for instance: "Hi and welcome! Today I'm going to do this type of reading, you can just relax, and I'm going to do my best. Please save questions until the end." In the future, working as a medium, you may find yourself doing five to ten readings on the same day.

Then, it's good to have your introduction before every client, so they know what to expect. After six or seven back-to-back readings, it's easy to forget that the person in front of you may have zero knowledge of mediumship or of what to expect. So by having a small introduction, we can attune the client to the right expectations. They may not know that you are about to make contact with their father in the spirit world. They may have a completely different picture of a reading, so make sure to explain this before you start.

Step 5: Myths & Beliefs

We will now enter step five of this course; I hope you have had a chance to look at both the psychometry and psychic reading exercises as these will give you a deeper understanding of what we will be talking about in this step. I know some students like to read through the course and then go back and do the exercises—whether you do this is entirely up to you. But the further forward we go, the more often I will ask you to "feel" what we are doing, which will be easier if you do the exercises parallel to the course steps.

Are you ready to be a medium?

So, this is what I call the serious part. Of course, this whole course is serious, and mediumship is a very real and serious thing. But throughout the process, we aim to have a relaxed and playful attitude towards the subject. This part is basically the important stuff to know about yourself throughout the development process. Mediumship is like life. It's serious, but we should not take it "too seriously." In mediumship, you could say that being serious means being responsible, kind, professional, and using a lot of common sense. You are intuitive and intelligent—you need to feel your clients and be honest about who you can help and who you can't. Readings are not for everyone. Some people need other forms of help, and you must point them in the right direction. I want to give you some good advice from my own experience. If a client can't stop talking during the reading, you are not the right person for them unless you are a certified therapist. Stop the reading and say, "I'm sorry, I can't get a connection for you today." End of story. It is not a matter of hiding from responsibility, this is actually being highly responsible. If someone comes to a healer's office with a broken leg, the healer hopefully sends them to the hospital.

We are working with the spirit, the soul, and of course our clients can be sad and lost in their lives, which is why they seek guidance, and we can help them with that. But we don't fix broken minds. We don't get involved in a client's mental drama or psychological issues—that's a job for therapists or psychiatrists. Our clients need to have a basic amount of emotional and mental health to benefit from a reading.

Suppose you see a poster or an ad for a mediumship demonstration or something similar. In this case, if you read the bottom of that poster, you will likely find "for entertainment purposes only." It may sound strange, but that phrase has a point. I'm not saying that mediumship is just entertainment; it's much more. I'm saying that the client needs to have that type of relaxed expectation. The client needs to be wise and sensible enough to handle the information in a healthy way. They need to have the strength and self-responsibility to enjoy the reading and discard all the information you have given them if they don't like or agree with it.

This is obvious and common sense for most developing mediums, and this is what I talk about when I say we take mediumship seriously but not "too seriously." We accept both the possibilities and the limitations in what we do. Most of our clients share our interest in the spirit world, and, like us, they want to explore the possibility of connecting to their loved ones in spirit. It's all done in love and light. And at the end of the day, they go on with their everyday lives with a little more love in their hearts, knowing their loved ones in spirit are with them.

If all of this resonates, you probably have a healthy picture of mediumship. But if you think your job as a medium is more than I have described here, if you feel like "a medium is a spiritual person's therapist," then you need to ask yourself a few questions. Why do you want to do this? Why do you want to develop your mediumship? Why do you think your knowledge and life experiences would benefit your client? Once again, I'm not judging anyone here. I'm saying this because I see it all the time. A mother in spirit comes through and says, "My son has problems in his relationship," and the medium says: "Dump her!!" No, the mother didn't say this, she just wanted you to shine light on her son and confirm that she knows what's happening. But it's the son's responsibility to handle the situation. You are there to make the connection, not to deliver the solution. I hope you understand my point. If someone wants a new car and you don't see a new car, then that's the information.

And most importantly, it's very common for a medium to pick up on a client's health, especially if it's bad. But if a client asks or has concerns about their health, an ongoing illness or disease, you tell them to go to the doctor. You don't dig into it; it's not your job. Simply point them in the right direction without scaring them: "Sorry, I can't help you with that. That's a question for your doctor."

As we talked about earlier, mediumship comes from the heart. The connection to the spirit or a client is a heart-based exercise where we listen to our clairs and deliver the information with common sense, lovingly, and responsibly. Anything else is drama, mental energy, and a need to feel important or superior to another person. When mediumship is done right, the client feels as if you were never in the room. They feel like they had a pleasant or healing conversation with a relative or loved one in spirit. When mediumship is done wrong, it's usually because the medium took too much space during the reading and made themself too important. All this can sometimes be a very thin line, and I want to give you an example from my work to illustrate what I mean. If I shoot a TV episode, I know that it's made for entertainment because that's what TV is. I know that much of the focus will be on me and my skills as a medium; it's inescapable. But when the cameras start, my job is to create a bubble around the client and their loved ones from the spirit world. This means I must remind myself to put my bags at the door, leave myself outside, and not get involved in the entertainment drama. TV production is big hectic machine with many people, but if I get too involved, I will start listening more to my brain than my clairs, and then I'm not being professional or doing my job as a medium.

I hope this section has given you some food for thought. I bring this up, like I said, not to judge anyone, but to help you in your development. Mediumship done the right way with the right intentions benefits both you and your clients. Developing a healthy and humble approach to mediumship will open your eyes in your personal life and send positive ripples to people and situations around you. I want you to be on the right path from the beginning, so when you uncover your skills and confidence as a medium, you will be able to do fantastic work for many people.

There is nothing to fear

Once upon a time, over twenty years ago, I did the license training and took the certificate for skydiving. I bought all this expensive equipment; the suit, the helmet, and the parachute. And for about four summers, my friend and I went to this local airstrip and jumped out of small planes. This was at a time in my life when I was still searching hard on the outside for the ultimate experience. I was willing to try anything to get my adrenaline going, and I absolutely loved it! But I wrestled with a lot of fears, too. Once I got the right amount of experience, the fear subsided and was replaced with confidence. The funny thing is that the things I feared had nothing to do with the actual skydiving. Skydiving is a very developed and straightforward process, and my fears were just small things I had squeezed in here and there for no reason. My only fears were in the morning or in the car to the airstrip, once we were up in the sky and the door was open, these fears were long gone.

The same goes for mediumship, a very developed and straightforward process with many nooks and crannies for people to squeeze in fears and doubts. Some people do it, others don't. You probably know how you feel about this stuff. So just to make it clear, if the words "fear" and "doubt" *don't* resonate with you when it comes to mediumship, that's excellent. If they *do*, know that it's very normal and absolutely okay. Stuff like this is built in to the human mind; it's a matter of self-preservation. Our minds tend to be overprotective before we have sufficient knowledge about a particular subject. And when it comes to these "spiritual things" such as mediumship, which is experienced through a new set of senses (the clairs), it can sometime takes a bit of time before we're able to let go of fears and doubts.

I want to tell you a common experience for someone starting on their mediumistic development journey, and I'm going to make this a metaphor. So just follow my story here.

Imagine you had never seen a swimming pool in your life, not in real life and not in a picture. You didn't know what it was. You had heard other people talk about it, and in your mind, you had created this mental concept of what it was, a concept based on a very limited experience. The only thing you knew for sure was that you wished to see a swimming pool and have the experience of diving into one. (I know this is a very abstract example, but stay with me.)

So, you work all year and save up some vacation money. When summer arrives and you get a couple weeks vacation from work, you decide it's time to make the swimming pool dream come true. No one around you understands your deep interest in swimming pools, so you decide to book a vacation and go alone to a luxurious hotel in Miami. This hotel has everything anyone could wish for, including an award-winning indoor pool area. (There are still no pictures, you just read in the brochure that they have a pool.) Then, the day comes and you fly to Miami. You check in to this hotel, and due to some extraordinary circumstances, you get upgraded to the suite on the tenth floor. Very nice! You go up there, order some room service, and go to bed because tomorrow you plan to wake up early to go to the swimming pool. It's hard to fall asleep because just the thought of it excites you.

When you wake the following day, you have a quick room-service breakfast, put on your swimming suit, take a bathrobe and a towel and head out to the elevator. Once you get into the elevator, you see all the buttons from the tenth to first floors are labeled "Lobby." Beneath the lobby button, there is a button for the indoor parking area, and then, all the way down, at the bottom, there is a button labeled "Pool Area." Fantastic! It's finally going to happen! You press the "Pool Area" button, the doors close, and you start to go down (this is a very slow elevator). On the seventh floor, the elevator stops, and another person gets in. This person presses the "Lobby Button," the doors close, and you start going downwards together. After a while (in this very slow elevator), the other person looks at all the buttons, sees which one you have pressed, and says,

"You're not going to the pool area, are you!?"

And you say, "Yes, I am!"

This person looks at you with big eyes and says, "I wouldn't do that if I were you, it's dangerous. There are sharks in that pool." Stunned, you look at this person, and before you can say anything, the elevator stops at the lobby, and they get out.

Now you are having second thoughts. This fascinating and exciting "swimming pool thing" that you have in your head is starting to crumble, and you wonder if you made the wrong decision. The doors close again, and the elevator starts moving. Now, suddenly, you don't know what to do and are trying to think fast. Should you press the "Parking Area" button and get out of there or press the "Emergency Stop" button? But before you have had time to decide what to do, the door opens, and you are now on the bottom floor, the pool area. You stay in the elevator for a while before peeking outside the elevator doors. And there, outside the elevator, you see a long hallway. At the end of this hallway is a large sign with a bright sun and a big arrow with the text: "Pool Area." What are you going to do now? You muster up your courage and step out of the elevator.

You have traveled too far and waited too long not to at least have a little peek. You just can't accept that the concept in your head and the exciting feelings you always had about this could be so wrong.

Slowly, you walk down this hallway, not knowing what to expect. You begin to think that if there *are* sharks in there, at least they won't be able to jump out into the hallway. So as long as you stay far away from the pool, you should be fine, right? Now, you get to the sign with the sun and the big arrow, and suddenly you hear people talking and laughing. You hear the water splashing; it doesn't sound all that dangerous. So, you peek around the next corner and see the whole pool area. You see people swimming and kids playing in the water. On one side, there are people getting massages, and on the other, there is a nice juice bar where people are sitting in their bathrobes talking and reading newspapers. Being a little skeptical about the pleasant atmosphere, you muster up even more courage and start to walk into the pool area. It feels pretty good, and you feel more confident with every step.

Suddenly, you are standing at the edge of the pool. You are just inches from the water. You can now see the whole pool. You see everything. And without a doubt, you know that there are no sharks in the pool. How could there be sharks in the pool? It's a pool!! You take off the bathrobe, dive into the water, and never look back.

So what's the moral of this story? The moral is this: once you have experienced real mediumship, you know, without a shadow of a doubt, that there is nothing to fear. The spirit world consists of pure, loving souls. Souls that once stepped into the body of a newborn child and then returned to the same loving state when that human being's time was over. They may talk about all the flaws and hardships during their lifetime here on earth, but they take no anger, resentment, or blame with them to the other side. All the problems or attitude issues they may have had in their lifetime were produced in their brains and physical minds. They were not born bad or evil and didn't return that way to the other side. Similarly, the most hard-boiled criminal on earth will still come through on a link of love. They may talk about all the awful things they did, and your clairs may pick this up as negative feelings. But there is nothing negative there; it's just communication. And in cases like this, they almost always wish to ask your client for forgiveness and tell them they love them.

As you continue on your development path and experience the truth of the "other side," this loving point of view will become your experience. But know this: there will always be people in the elevator on your way there. People that tell you stuff they don't know anything about. And they will never know because they will never muster up the courage to go to the pool area—they will always get off at the lobby.

Step 6: Divination & Mediumship

In the last step, we talked about the serious parts of mediumship, and we can summarize it like this: use common sense and base your beliefs on your own experiences, not someone else's. I also hope you are doing the exercises and have checked off a couple of them on the exercise sheet. Soon, we will introduce some new exercises, and it'll be good if you have finished the psychometry and psychic reading exercises by then. And, of course, keep doing the stillness exercise every day if you can. If you complete the thirty stillness exercises on the exercise sheet before you finish the course, then just keep doing them every day until the end.

In this step, we will talk about "divination." In divination, we use a tool to gain knowledge or information about a specific subject, a person's life, or, most commonly, the future.

This tool can be anything from a card deck to a pendulum, colored ribbons, runes, coffee beans, crystal balls, etc.

Divination

Divination is not an absolute necessity on your development journey. You can do without it and obtain the same results in your mediumship. I put it into this course because so many people are interested in the subject. A deck of cards, such as angel or tarot cards, are often the first thing that enters a person's life when they start their mediumship journey. If you do it right, it's also exciting and fun because a deck of cards, or any other divination tool, may seem to speak to you differently than just reading "empty space." I don't use these types of tools when working with my clients, but I use them with students and for fun when I'm with like-minded friends. Divination, especially cards, is also something that works well if you want to practice alone, as it stimulates your clairs even if there is no one else in the room. I always tell my students that if there is ever a slow period in your development process and you don't have time to work so much on your mediumship, it's always good to have something that can stimulate your senses and clairs. Having a deck of cards somewhere close is an easy and fast way to dust off your clairs.

You could just pull a card in the morning, see what you draw, and then see if that morning insight comes through during the day.

How does it work?

To clarify this, I will focus on just card decks, but the same goes for any divination tool. If you can read a deck of cards, you can apply this skill to anything. You can read tea leaves, Turkish coffee, or a bowl of M&Ms. Focusing on cards for this example, I can explain it as follows: the "magic" is not in the cards, the "magic" is in you. It feels like I have used this phrase earlier in the course, but it doesn't matter; it's still just as true. Cards are just cards, pretty pictures printed on nice paper—nothing more and nothing less. Even if you visited the sacred city of Machu Picchu and found a golden card deck wrapped in five-thousand-year-old silk, it would still be just a card deck. The simple explanation is one we have already gone through in this course; all readings are you reading energy. What the card deck does is stimulating the clairs. The pictures distract the mind, the ongoing mental process, and suddenly the clairs become much louder. The cards distract your logical brain and puts you in the right place to hear, see, or feel your clairs. What you are doing is the same as in psychometry. You let an object (in this case, a card) speak to you through your clairs. It doesn't matter which card deck you use or what's on the picture, as the information usually has nothing to do with this if done correctly. The same picture should be able to give you different information depending on who you are doing the reading for. A card filled with "gold bars" doesn't mean "unexpected income" for every client every time you pull it.

I'm aware that some people probably disagree with this definition of divination. They want to underline that some card decks, the right card decks, have their own energy and magic. And in this case, it's up to you to decide what you believe. Is your natural-born sixth sense only half of the equation in mediumship, or can you do just fine with no tools? For me, the answer is simple. The fact is that cards or any other tool can be used for both psychic and mediumistic readings, and people who are very visual or "clairvoyant" can find them very useful. But there comes the point when you need to be independent of any tool to do your readings. If you, for example, always work with cards and use them all the time, your body and your whole development process becomes very dependent on them. It will become hard to do all the different types of readings that we have talked about. In this course, I want to teach you to become a medium able to do all types of readings, either with or without tools. I don't want to teach you to become a tarot reader. There is absolutely nothing wrong with being a tarot reader and many of them do fantastic work, but in this course, I don't want to limit you to a specific type of reading—I want you to master them all. Then, when you have mastered your mediumship skills, you are free to specialize in any area you wish to.

The reason I'm being so clear about my personal opinion on this subject is because, in my work with students, I have seen how these different types of tools sometimes limit students. It hinders their development, and they feel a little naked working without their tool. They come to me wishing to take the next step in their development process, and when I ask them to do a reading exercise, they say: "If I had my cards here, I could've done it." They have placed too much confidence in the tool and don't believe they can do it without them.

How to do it

That said, I'm going to teach you how to read cards because soon you'll be doing the divination exercise in this course. I want you to master this type of reading while not feeling dependent on any tool. We will focus on cards here, but if you have some other type of tool that you feel speaks to you and your clairs, you are also free to use them. There are many different card decks: tarot, angel cards, oracle cards, color cards, mandala cards, Lenormand cards, and many more. I think I have about twenty-five different card decks, but most have never been used. So, you shuffle the cards, take a few, and put them on the table in front of you. In tarot language, this is called a "spread," and there are many types of specific spreads depending on what you or the client are asking for (which you don't need to learn to be a medium). As always, it isn't important how you do this, pull as many cards as you like and put them any way you want. Let's say you put three cards in front of you and, starting from the left, you decide to name the cards past, present, and future. What you are subconsciously doing here is telling your clairs where on the client's timeline to focus. If you switch and say past, present, future, but from the right instead, it would be the same.

With the three cards in front of you, just relax. Don't try to interpret what's on the pictures, just look at them like gazing out over a sunset, and you will start to activate your clairs. Then say the first thing that comes up, a feeling, a word, a picture, or just something you "know." Let the cards be there just as a colorful distraction for your eyes as you start looking inwards, scanning your clairs. Then continue the reading the same way as you would in any other type of reading. If the reading and the information get a good momentum going, you can put the cards to one side, since they have done their job. They have distracted your brain enough to switch focus, and the information will continue by itself. Just like art, interior design, or colors generally speak differently to different people, so do different card decks. When using cards for a reading, make sure that you have a card deck that feels appealing to your visual senses. If you have never used card decks before, choose a light, colorful, and uplifting deck, making it easier to stimulate the playful attitude needed to do a reading. Some decks are a little too doom and gloom, which only stimulates mental drama. Like everything else we do, we must do this with a feeling of joy.

This is the way I define and teach the art of card reading. And of course, just like the earlier subjects, such as chakras and the aura, this too is something you can dive deeper into if you are interested. There are thousands of books on tarot and divination. But like I said, it's good to know how it works as it's a good tool for development, but it's not an essential part of your future work as a medium.

Mediumship

We have already talked a bit about mediumship in previous steps, considering the theory, how it works, and the differences between intuition, psychic, and mediumistic energy. Now we will try to find words for the actual experience or feeling part of mediumship. I will probably repeat some of the stuff we have already talked about, but the answers are always in the basics, and any repetition of the material will only do you good.

By now, I hope you have had the time to do the stillness exercise for a while. And if you have, you may start to notice that the exercise, or the experience, has changed from the first time you did it. It probably feels more relaxed now, and there is less stuff happening when you do it. You can still be swept away on some journey, but everything should begin to slow down a little. Any overwhelming symbolic imagery should start to fade. If you feel this change is happening for you, good. If you don't feel this change, it's still okay—you just need to continue doing the exercise a little longer. This change in the stillness exercise means your mental activity has slowed down, and you have shifted your frequency. You have left your bags at the door and are now in the right place, waiting for the calling card, the sign from our guide telling us they are there and ready to work with us. This is your starting point for any reading or mediumistic work.

Mediumship and communication with the spirit world have a purpose: to connect a person (your client) to their specific loved one in spirit. This means that when you are all alone doing the stillness exercise and get the feeling that "someone" is there with you, it's most likely your guide you are feeling. Sometimes, if you have booked a reading with a client, you may feel a spiritual contact that comes a little early, say ten minutes before the reading begins. That's okay, just say thanks and ask them to return when the reading starts. You are always in charge and always in control. But when you are alone, relaxing, or doing that type of development exercise, no random spirits will be flying around trying to talk to you. As a medium, you are the telephone, not the call's recipient. There's no conversation if there's no client on one end and spirit on the other. You are not walking around randomly talking to the spirit world, and the spirit world is not following you because you are a medium. The spirits are like most living people—we rarely focus on those we don't know.

So when you are alone or with your guide, and you have opened up and are in the right place, there is not much else you have to do. Your guide is working with you, but most of it is behind the scenes, helping you with your energy and fine-tuning your frequency. Usually, you don't notice this, it's just a pleasant, relaxing experience. You can step out of it anytime by standing up and continuing with your everyday life. Sometimes we may feel a little lightheaded after exercises or readings. This is our frequency adjusting back to normal life.

When you are with a client and intend to connect to the spirit world, the spirit can come through. If you have prepared yourself, and your client is there specifically to be part of the reading, the spirit will know this. I have found the closest way to describe the feeling of connecting to someone's loved one in spirit is a feeling like you are making it up. It feels abstract, and sometimes too easy to be true. It's like: "I'm seeing this lady in my mind, and she feels old. For some reason, she's showing me her old hands?" Well, you don't have to make sense of what's happening. Give the information to your client, and there is a big possibility that they know exactly what it means. This is why I go on and on about having a playful attitude. When you do the reading in a loving, lighthearted, and explorational way, you are much closer to the energy of the spirit world. It will be much easier to accept that it's happening; you are speaking to the spirit world. This connection, or this moment, is way too often approached like a religious ceremony. People or mediums think it has to get all heavy and serious before we deserve the presence of the other side. Do you hear how religious this argument sounds? There's nothing wrong with being religious or approaching it like a religious ceremony, you are free to choose what path you walk through life. But mediumship is not religion, they are two separate things. There are atheists, skeptics, and people in prison who have a fantastic gift of mediumship, and that's because the spirit world has no criteria to meet before being allowed to communicate. We are souls incarnated in these bodies, and the spirit world is made up of these same souls. They are just not in a physical body right now. What we do is communicate, soul to soul, just as we speak person to person. For example, imagine someone's old uncle Jim, who was in the police force, loved football, and liked to drink a couple of beers. He was always joking and made people around him feel really good, but he never went to church even once his whole life. How would he like you, as a medium, to approach him? In the same way as he was when living.

It's not about waiting for the day you are holy or pure enough to deserve this gift. It's about going after it repeatedly, realizing that they want you to communicate their love to their friends and relatives who are still here on earth. What if you get some of the information wrong in the beginning? They're not going to give up on you. You have already proven yourself worthy of the spirit world by sitting with your client and intending to make a spiritual connection. My old mentor used to say, "It all starts on the platform," which means: go for it! Be prepared and put yourself in a situation where the client is really hoping to make contact with that loved one in spirit, and they will come. Then, you just say what your clairs are telling you.

Okay, so this is my way of trying to put words to the experience of mediumship. And as you can see, we always wrestle back and forth between mediumistic development and limiting beliefs. I'm trying to show you the not-so-complicated part of mediumship and, at the same time, trying to shed light on how complicated we make it by believing it to be. I'm also using phrases like "other people" and "other mediums," which are not specific people or mediums. These phrases are used to provide reflections of ourselves so we can see the difference between how we see things, and how we now need to see things differently to get results. We need to peel off the beliefs stuck on that velcro ball, the core of mediumship, and simplify, not complicate, the process. So, from now on, I want you to adopt an attitude of, "No matter what, I'm just going to go for it. If I'm wrong or if my readings get flooded by the white marbles in my mind, I'm just going to go on." There will come a day when you will have done a hundred readings, and then you will be awestruck by the simplicity of the process.

Exercise 4 | Divination

In the section about divination, we mainly talked about working with cards as a tool. If possible, even if you are already using some other type of divination tool, I would like you to use cards for this exercise. It doesn't matter which type of cards you use, you could use an ordinary deck of playing cards. If you can get a deck of tarot or oracle cards, these will be more stimulating for your visual senses.

How to do it

Begin by doing your little start-up routine and then the first half of the stillness exercise. When you are ready, invite the client into the room or contact your client if you are on Skype or telephone. Do a three-card spread before you and decide which card is past, present, and future. Then, relax and listen to your clairs. What is your body telling you? Remember, we do this as a psychic exercise with the intention of tuning in to the client's energy. If you should get the feeling that someone else, like a spirit contact, is there when you read the client's energy, just thank them and ask them to come back some other time. They won't be offended, quite the opposite. It's a good sign that shows you are in charge of your work. Then, shift your focus back to your client and keep listening to your clairs. Say the first thing that comes to mind, and let the information guide you. If you get stuck, look at the cards. It's not super important that you stick to the past-present-future thing. If the reading takes another direction, go with it. If you need to pull more cards from the deck, do it. Follow your clairs and build upon the subtle story the cards tell you. When you finish, thank your client and ask them to email you some feedback. Then do the second half of the stillness exercise, and you are done.

If you feel I'm not being super-detailed about how to work with your cards, it's because I don't want you to worry about doing the right or wrong thing. They are just a tool. If they seem to positively affect your reading, great. If not, just continue listening to your clairs.

Please do this exercise with four clients for twenty minutes each. You should do the full twenty minutes no matter what, and during the reading, ask the client to be silent. Of course, you can ask them if they understand what you are talking about, if they recognize a person or a specific object or situation, to reassure you that you are making sense. But any questions should be based on the information you have already delivered. If you ask your client a question, instruct them to answer yes or no rather than a "fill the blanks" style answer. The reading should never turn into a conversation. If the client desperately wants to tell you something about what you have picked up, they can do so after the reading or in the feedback email. It would also be best not to use the same clients for different exercises as we did initially. I want you to experience "feeling" other people's energy. So, get four new clients for this exercise, and in the upcoming exercises, you will be required to get new clients again. If you do this course with a friend, you can help each other. You may have other friends who want a reading, but as you likely know them too well, it's best to switch and do readings for each other's friends.

Exercise 5 | Stretched Psychic Reading

The stretched psychic reading exercise is where we look a little further for contact in the spirit world. As you will soon notice, all these exercises are linked and build upon the experience from those before it. You are going to do the same thing you did in the psychic reading exercise, but this time you are going to focus on "the other side" (there are no cards in this exercise).

How to do it

I call this a stretched psychic reading because the psychic information from your client's energy will still be much stronger and easier to link to, and you will be tempted to start reading and talking about the client. But there are some key differences: you can still read the client, but now and then, I want you to feel, see, or hear whether someone else is with you. And if you are not sure, ask your client. For example, "Do you know an old fisherman on the other side?" (if that is what you are picking up). If they say no, just continue with the psychic part. Then, after a while, look again to see if someone is there. "Do you recognize an old lady in a wheelchair on the other side?" If your client says yes, then shift your focus and try to get more information about that lady.

During this exercise, you will likely get it wrong. There will be a lot of white marbles sneaking in, and your mind will try to force you to interpret and make sense of what you are feeling and seeing. But try just to give exactly what you get. The information may not be coherent, and your reading may jump all over the place. That's okay, keep going. This exercise is a bit longer; I want you to do five clients for thirty minutes each. If you feel you are just babbling on and the client doesn't know what you are talking about, keep on going and do the entire thirty minutes.

You will be more relaxed with each time you do this exercise, and the information will get a little clearer. You have already done and are familiar with most parts of this exercise. You open up and close down the same way we always do, through the stillness exercise. The only difference is that you need to keep looking for that spirit, that contact, just waiting to talk and say hello to their loved one, your client.

When you are finished with this exercise, we will enter some fascinating parts of this course and everything we have done so far will lead up to this next step. We will put the psychic and intuitive stuff aside for a while and start to focus purely on communicating with the spirit. If you have a lot of unfinished exercises from previous steps in the course, please try to get them all done—it will serve you well as we move on to the next steps of the course.

Step 7: Structure Your Readings

This step is about the structure we use to link and work with the spirit, and from now on, we will focus predominantly on spirit work. We have already touched on this subject in previous steps and exercises, and now I want to guide you step-by-step through a reading and show you the blueprint of making one come together, and how to make a reading feel like a whole and polished experience. I'm also going to approach this with less of a student feel because if you've done all the previous exercises, this is the step or "threshold" I talked about at the beginning of the course. It's time to let go of the training wheels and step into your power as a medium.

So before we open the door and "link" with the spirit, we first need to do a couple of things to create a friendly, relaxed, and professional atmosphere. We have already begun making connections in the stretched psychic reading exercise, but here I am purely talking about a direct mediumship reading to connect with spirits. Another difference is that in earlier exercises, we were very clear about the "being a student" part. We made sure to tell our clients this so we could relax and lower the expectations a little. But now, we need to stop pulling the student card and present ourselves as mediums. No matter how good or bad our future readings are, we will stand up for ourselves and just own the experience. If we give someone a great reading, we will keep the pride to ourselves and keep working, knowing that we did a good, professional job. If we give someone a terrible reading, we will own that experience too, and won't beat ourselves up or apologize for it. Tell yourself, "I did my best, it didn't go the way I wanted, but I'll keep working on it," and then move on to the next client.

Of course, I know that you are a student and still at an early stage in your mediumistic career. But I want you to get over the threshold during this course, not after it. I want you to do it now, with me, so I can help and guide you before you get the chance to pull any brakes. You are a medium already; by taking this step, you could become a fantastic one, and that's my goal for you.

How to structure a professional reading

First, like always, we have the startup routine: relaxing, maybe lighting a candle, and then the first half of the stillness exercise. This part we always do before any reading. Then it's time for the introduction, which we looked at earlier. I want you to get your introduction right from the beginning. If you need to write it down and practice it, do it. In this example, I will describe the situation as if you were sitting face to face in the same room as your client. Later, you can adjust this to fit both Skype and telephone readings.

An example of an introduction that I do before a reading would be the following. After we have said hello and shook hands, we sit down, and I always ask just one question before the reading: "Have you done this before?" That's a yes or no question. I don't want them to start talking. If they have never done this before, I need to clarify my introduction. Because of my personal style and my down-to-earth approach to mediumship, I tend to get a lot of first-timers. That's because first-timers usually want the experience without too much "woo-woo"; that's the truth. And then, I pick up my voice recorder and ask if they wish to have the reading recorded. If they say yes, I do so, and they will get a link in their email within three days to a secure audio download site. I do readings for a couple of days, after which I send all the audio files out on the following Monday. The recording is included in the price, clearly explained on the website. Ninety-nine percent of clients want this recording. I always start the recorder before the introduction so no one can say they didn't know what they were getting themselves into. If they don't like the introduction, they can end the reading free of charge.

Continuing

If they have never done a reading or been to a medium before, I start by explaining that all mediums work differently and that a reading can be done in many different ways. I explain that I work with spirit contact and that these spirits will be people they know: family, friends, and loved ones that have passed over to the other side. So now they don't have to worry about me talking about guides or random spirits; the contact will be connected to them. I'm always very honest about the whole process, and I tell them that sometimes it doesn't work, but I will do my best to give them a good reading. I keep the mystique of the process down at zero. I also acknowledge that the client may have some questions, and I instruct them to keep these until later in the reading. I will do the mediumistic part of the reading first. Then, after maybe thirty minutes, I will switch and focus on the client and continue with psychic energy. This is usually a better place to let the client ask their questions as most are generally connected to their life, here and now.

And I know that in this course, we separate psychic readings from mediumistic readings, but that's for educational purposes. In the future, when your clients know how you work, you can develop your style and do both types of readings in the same session. But in the beginning, when you are just starting out, it's easier to get clients if you separate the two types of readings into two different services on, for example, your website.

The reading starts

So here we go, the reading starts, and all focus is on the clairs and finding a contact in spirit. Observe the first thing that comes: a picture, a feeling, a person, a uniform, a car, a horse, whatever. Then I build on that feeling, person, or picture. Because I have done a couple thousand readings by now, I have worked out a system with the spirit world, so they will appear in a particular place depending on their connection to the client. My left, the client's right, is the father's side. And my right, the client's left, is the mother's side. Upwards are the older people, and downwards are the younger people. In front of the client, below their knees, are the kids who are alive. So now, a grandmother can point down and talk about one of her grandkids. I know this sounds a little advanced in the beginning, but I'm telling you this because over time you will find those same people, such as grandmothers, appear on the same side or in the same place for every client. And there you have a lot of free and accurate information. Instead of just "an old lady," you will say, "I've got your grandmother here." And just to clarify, when I say they "appear," I'm talking about a subjective picture or feeling that they are on a specific side of my client. They don't physically appear.

Now the spirit contact is there, and I can start communicating with them. As you can see, there is a pretty worked-out structure to everything we do before, during, and after the reading. This is not to complicate things but to keep you and the spirit world on the same page every step of the way. If they know your structure, and you stick to it, they will know when it's time for them to jump in. They know when you are "listening" to them. Now, your energies meet and blend at the same time. When I say I start to communicate with them, I also do this using a specific structure, which the whole next section will focus on in terms of communication. If they already know your first couple of questions, they can answer them much faster and clearer.

So, back to the reading. You have now talked to the grandmother, and that contact feels finished. The client is both happy and emotional. Then you ask the grandmother (silently in your mind), "Who else is up there?" And the next spirit contact comes through. You will most likely fall out of the link many times initially, meaning that you feel you have lost contact. If that happens, wait and listen to your clairs, and the link will build up again. After about thirty minutes, it will feel normal to switch over to the client's energy and start talking about them and their lives and answering any questions. When the reading is finished, you thank them and stop the recorder. They pay and leave, and you close down using the second part of the stillness exercise.

So that's a reading, and if you (at least in the beginning) stick to this structure, you will notice everything go much smoother, and the client will see you as a professional medium.

How to structure your evidence

In the last section, we talked about how to structure a reading and the steps we need to take to make the whole experience feel professional to the client. With structure comes confidence, and you relax more when you know what to do. In this section, we continue to talk about structure, but this time, we will focus on the structure of the actual information we deliver.

In the headline, you can see that I have used the word "evidence," a word that has become the go-to in many mediumistic books, courses, and workshops. Evidence is commonly used in the spiritualist tradition, in which we say we work with "evidence or proof of life after death." Another good thing about this word for us as mediums is that it sets the bar a little higher, making it easier for us to determine whether we are giving the client clear evidence or information. And there is a big difference there. "I have got a lady here with me," that's information. "I have got your one-legged grandmother here," that's evidence. I'm not saying that the "information" in this example is wrong. You may, at the moment, just have "a lady" there. But you want to build on that contact. You want that information to become specific enough that it's evident to the client that it's their grandmother. And you accomplish this by structuring the evidence.

By using the routines and structures we talked about in the last section, we now control the outer environment of the reading and it will progress the way we want it to. Then, we enter the "right place," the "bubble" of spirit communication where everything can be very unstructured—a very creative, and subtle bubble of different information jumping from one clair to the next. We want to apply the same structure within this "bubble" as we have on the outside. And we do this by asking the spirit working with us questions. Questions are the difference between information and evidence. You ask these questions silently in your mind, "Who are you? Give me something specific." You don't let the client be a part of this process; they only get the evidence coming through your clairs.

So here is the structure that I recommend, and if you follow this and always ask these questions (one at a time, silently in your mind) in every contact with a spirit, you will find they learn and accept the way you work, and they will answer these questions for you. After each question, give the answer/evidence to your client.

Question #1: "Okay, spirit, who's here?" You get the communicator and make a connection with this spirit contact. This is also called "connecting with the spirit."

Question #2: "Please describe yourself." Here, you describe the communicator. How does this person look? Tall, small, thin, fat? What's their eye-color or hairstyle? Any beard or tattoos?

Question #3: "How did you pass over/die?" Was it by illness, accident, or old age? Feel your clairs. If they were sick, where in the body did this happen? Heart, lungs, head?

Question #4: "Please tell me HOW you were." You are looking for personality traits here. How does this spirit contact feel? Like a happy, shy, or stubborn person?

Question #5: "Who are you?" How is this spirit contact connected to your client? Grandmother, friend, or maybe an old school teacher?

Question #6: "Please tell me some memories." Here, you are looking for a memory that connects this spirit contact with your client: "We played football together," or "She married my brother."

And finally, Question #7: "Why are you here?" This is the message, the reason the spirit contact has come through today.

A message is often very loving and can come through different clairs simultaneously. A mother in spirit can send a feeling of love and, at the same time, a picture of the client's old teddy bear. It can be a message of forgiveness, or maybe the spirit saying, "I was there at your wedding," or "I was there when you gave birth." The message is often very cozy, but still evidential. Sometimes, the message can also be a "loving kick in the butt," such as a father in spirit saying, "Move on, you are the boss of your own life." And sometimes, the client and the spirit contact didn't get along in life, so the spirit respectfully steps back a little, and the message can feel a bit colder and more like a "gentle first step towards forgiveness." The message will NOT be "Quit your job, take the children, and divorce your husband." These types of choices in life are up to the individual human being to handle, and the spirit world doesn't interfere with our paths in life or our challenges towards growth. They can acknowledge this stuff is happening in the client's life or relationships, but they don't step in and decide for us.

So that's how to structure your evidence, and the seven questions you should use to ensure your reading and contact are building in the right direction. The contact is normally finished when you have gone through these questions and gotten the answers from spirit. All the important evidence has now been given to the client, so you can move on and see if there is some other spirit who wants to come through. You can then start from the beginning of the questions again. For some readings, you do one contact and for others, you may do four to five.

I hope this makes sense and doesn't feel like too much or too complicated. All this structure we have been talking about here and in the last section is something you won't even think about once you get some experience. The actual structure will be like riding a bike, guiding you from the back of your mind. You will feel free to relax and improvise or change anything at any moment. The structure also gives the reading its momentum, a feeling of forward motion. After twenty or thirty readings, this structure will start to sync with the time-frame you have set for the reading. You will find yourself finishing the reading at exactly the right time before your next client.

That's it! If you feel these last two sections have been much to take in, please read them again. Take notes and study them. Soon we will do all we have learned here by applying all these structures to the next exercise, the "mediumship" exercise. But before doing that, we will talk a little about staying focused.

Stay focused

Previously, we talked about how to structure communication with the spirit world to get the best possible evidence. We are now building up to the next and final exercise: mediumship readings. Because I have put so much emphasis on this exercise in the previous two sections, it may sound like we are going to do something completely new, but we are not. If you have done the earlier exercises in this course, this next one will likely feel similar. We will focus on the spirit world, and there will be a change in how we present ourselves to our clients. You are still a student, and it's okay to tell your clients this, but we will try not to pull the student card and use it as an excuse if a reading doesn't go as we wanted it to.

First, I want to talk a little more about focus, especially your role as a medium and where you should keep your focus when you are working. Of course, you will be focused when sitting with a client, it comes automatically with the situation. You will be very aware of the task you are about to perform and will probably be very focused on your actual link or connection. But the focus I'm talking about here is how you see yourself in this situation and how you handle this very important moment without making yourself too important. Let's do a small example.

Imagine yourself working as a nurse in a hospital. One late afternoon you walk into a patient's room, and this very old man is lying on his bed taking his last breaths. He moves his hand and asks you to come closer, then he whispers in your ear, "Please, tell my son I always loved him and that I'm sorry I never told him. Please tell him." And then he dies. I know this is a dramatic example. So, now the hospital calls the family, and one hour later, they are all there, gathered around this man's bed.

"Was anyone with him when he died?" His son, the man's only child, asks.

You, still in the room, raise your hand and say, "Yes, I was here with him."

Then son the says, "Did he say anything before he died?" Suddenly, you now have information that is super important in this situation, to the family, and especially to the man's son. At this moment, you are holding the key to possibly life-changing information. But still, you, as a person, are unimportant; this has nothing to do with you. You are a messenger. Your message will probably significantly impact the son's life, yet you and your role in this will soon be forgotten. That's the way it should be.

So how would you deliver this message to the son? "I think your father was talking a bit about this and a little about that. . . ." No, this would not be the way to do it. You should deliver the message word for word with utmost respect for the man, the son, and the situation. The son would thank you, and then your role in all of this would be over.

It's pretty easy to translate this to a mediumistic reading, which you have probably done already. The focus should be on mediumship, not on the medium. You deliver the information, word for word, as it comes through your clairs. If you do a good reading, fine! If you do a bad reading, fine! It's not about you. If you do the reading with the right focus and intention, then the outcome is what it is. The more experience you get, the better your readings will be. You are an important yet small piece in a much larger puzzle, and you can only develop and aim to control your part in the whole thing. Sometimes there are bigger, behind-the-scenes reasons, that we don't know about, and we can only trust that our current experience or result serves the highest good for all involved.

Exercise 6 | Mediumship

Finally! We have talked a lot about mediumship, and now it's time to do it. There are still a couple of essential steps left in this course, but this is the last planned exercise. This is in no way the end of this journey—it's the total opposite. When you have done these five readings, you will be on the springboard and on your way to mastering the art of mediumship. After these readings, the last pieces will fall into place, and you will feel, in your heart, that you are a medium and always have been. It's not a fluke or coincidence that you are reading this right now. It was always meant to be, and the space and energy needed for this course to happen were created long before you and me.

How to do it

The instructions for this exercise are simple: do it the way I taught you to do it, create the space, open up, structure your reading, focus on spirit contact, ask the questions, deliver what comes through your clairs, remember your role and focus as a medium, be professional but with a playful attitude, accept whatever happens, thank your client and ask them to email you some feedback, close down, move on. I want you to do five readings, thirty minutes long, each with a new client you haven't worked with before.

As a side note, earlier, I mentioned how I recorded my readings. You don't necessarily have to do this yet. There are a lot of pros and cons to recording your readings, which I'll talk about in the bonus section.

Okay, now go for it! Find your five clients, do your readings, and good luck!

Step 8: Working With Clients

So, last section was the mediumship exercise, and I hope you started it and had a chance to experience working with the structure of a reading and the evidence that comes with it. These exercises represent an important stepping stone in your development. As we move on, this exercise and type of mediumistic reading, working within this structure, will be our goal for future clients. Psychic abilities and divination tools will follow and become a natural part of the end of your readings, but from now on, we want to start each reading with a connection to spirit.

In this section, I want to talk about working with clients, particularly about the different types of clients that you may encounter in your work. Remember that I am talking about personality types, not "good" or "bad" clients, and absolutely no judgment is involved. Every person, reading, and connection to spirit is unique. But from my experience with my students and work, I know that clients tend to fall into certain categories. As a medium, you will pick up on this instantly. By knowing what type of client or personality type you have in front of you, you can approach the reading and work with the client in the best possible way to give them a positive experience.

For some, this may sound like a strange subject, talking about the client's personality. But if you look at the corporate world, for instance, they always do this. They even have tests for new employees to determine their personality. So why do they do that? To understand who they will be working with and to understand this person. Even though every person is unique, they are usually of a certain personality type.

By understanding who your client is, you can approach them in a way that makes them feel comfortable. They may be very shy, very nervous, or very skeptical. These factors can affect your focus and confidence, they can make you more mentally engaged in the situation and pull you out of the frequency needed to do the reading. And you, as a medium, also represent a personality type and will, over time, also be known as a certain type of medium. Some clients will be drawn to you, and some won't. For example, my personality may not fit every person reading this book, and that's okay, that's the way it is.

So, all clients have different levels of experience before making an appointment with you. They may also have had good or bad readings before, which will affect their expectations of you. As discussed earlier, some of them have "people in the elevator," friends or family who have helped them develop a slightly fear-based picture of this work. Some people just don't know why they are drawn to you, they have no previous experience, don't have any questions, and don't know why they are there. Whoever they are, it's okay. Keep your focus on your mediumship.

Different types of clients

Here is a general description of some personality types and the additional expectations for working with them.

Calm and nice

Most clients are just calm and friendly people. They come with an open mind and are just interested in the experience. They may hope for specific contact or a particular answer, but they are normally okay with whatever happens.

Skeptics

Some clients are openly skeptical about mediumship and usually tell you this before you start the reading. And a client with a healthy amount of skepticism is absolutely one-hundred-percent okay. It usually means they prefer to create their own picture of how life and the world works. They want a reading to see and maybe adjust this picture, but they don't want you to tell them what's real and what's not not—they want to figure that out for themselves. So, you just deliver the evidence, and then they are free to do whatever they want with it. I encourage people to use common sense and have healthy skepticism towards mediumship and all spiritual practices. I have even said it on TV. Our work is not to change people's beliefs. Never put yourself in a situation where you are arguing for what you believe in. Simply do your readings, deliver evidence, and let people decide for themselves what they do or don't believe. If a person is too skeptical, they usually don't book a reading.

"Professionals"

Then we have the "professionals," clients who go to readings all the time. They are usually very into mediumship, however they sometimes want you to confirm their beliefs rather than give them evidence. These readings also tend to pull a little more towards psychic stuff. Some "professional" clients openly say, "I'm not interested in the spirit contact." Instead, they want you to talk about them, which is also absolutely okay. Just make sure they don't start booking you for a reading every week, otherwise you might end up in a situation where the client expects you to make all their life decisions for them, and that's wrong. I usually don't see my clients more than once, and I ask them to wait at least a year if they want to return. The energies in their lives need to change, or they will get the same reading again.

Urgent clients

Some clients may contact you urgently, and often. These clients may have just lost someone. It's not unusual for someone to book a reading even before a friend's or loved one's funeral. The important thing to note here is that there is a time for grief and a time for readings. From my experience, once this spirit contact comes through, the client gets so emotional the spirit contact backs off, it's simply too painful for the client. If this happens, what you do is you stop the reading, explain that this is not the right time, and ask them to come back six to eight months later. The grief will have subsided a little by then, and the client will be able to enjoy a love-filled reading. These clients often bring jewelry, items, or pictures for you to do psychometry. If you prefer to do your readings without pictures or objects, that's okay, but you can still let them show it at the end of the reading because it's important to them.

Other mediums

Then we have one of the more challenging types of clients: other mediums. Or, more precisely, students of mediumship. For some reason, these clients sometimes come with a "know it all" attitude, and they tend to be more interested in correcting your evidence or pointing out when you are wrong. These clients are a fantastic opportunity for training yourself to remain focused and in the right frequency. Don't fall into the trap of letting yourself get sucked into some kind of drama. Stay professional, do your job, and you will automatically reflect their behavior back on them. They will see how far you have come on your development journey. And of course, this is not a general description of most mediumship students, most students who book readings are nice and eager to learn. This describes the few who have missed the mark and think mediumship is all about them.

A bit crazy . . .

And then, finally, we have clients who are a bit crazy. . . . We can't help these clients. We must say, nicely and politely, "Sorry, I can't get a connection for you," or "I don't think I'm the right medium to help you." Then we end the reading. No talking, no getting involved in their drama. And, of course, they don't pay. I have had clients come in with alarm clocks wrapped in tinfoil and Persian carpets soaked in vinegar. We can't help these clients. They need other forms of help. Luckily, these clients are pretty rare, and you can generally detect this when they contact you for a booking, so you can say no early on.

So, these are some of the "personalities" or "client types" you can expect when you work as a medium. Furthermore, a client can also be a mix of any or all of these personalities. Regardless of who walks in for a reading, as long as you aim to keep your focus and frequency in the right place, then everything will work out fine. If there are any problems, or if you are not comfortable with a client, just end the reading politely. Don't charge them any money, and let them go. And remember, we can't read all clients. Sometimes the energies between the medium and the client just don't work, no matter how friendly and polite your client is. In the future, you may have five readings booked on the same day. Two might go well, one might not work, and the last two might go well again. That's just the way it is. Your job is not to get hung up on the one reading that didn't work. Let it go and refocus on the next one.

Ethics and morals

So far, we have talked about working with clients, paying special attention to the different personality types you may encounter in your work. In this section, we will talk about ethics and morals, some "do's" and "dont's" in your work as a medium. We've mentioned many do's and dont's already, and I have deliberately inserted this information into the different steps in this course. But just to be sure, we will go through some of them again.

Never diagnose a client

Never "diagnose" a client or promise them anything connected to a disease or illness. First, it's not legal to diagnose somebody in most countries if you are not a licensed doctor or health care professional. And if you *are* a licensed doctor, you still shouldn't diagnose your clients during a reading. You do that wherever you work as a doctor. Sometimes, the line is very thin when it comes to questions about health, and clients can be very persuasive and say, "It's okay, just tell me." But please, don't go there. If they are sick in any way and ask for your help, tell them to go to the doctor.

Legally adult

In Sweden, you are legally an adult at eighteen, and I personally don't do readings for people any younger than this. Even if they are seventeen and very mature and wise, I ask them to return when they are eighteen. The client is responsible for how they choose to handle or interpret the evidence or information you give them but, if they are underage, this responsibility may backfire and land on you. Above the booking button on my website, it very clearly says there is an "18-year-age-limit on all services." If I do a demonstration at a bigger venue, the organizer or person selling the tickets is responsible, because I can't ask fifty people for their IDs before starting.

Clients have to book their reading

Clients should always book their own reading. Sometimes, someone who has been to you for a reading previously may want to gift a reading as a present to their husband or wife. This is, of course, very nice of them, and you may get emails asking if you have any nicely-designed gift certificates they can give away. They are welcome to pay for someone else's reading if they want to give this as a present, but the client, the actual person who is coming to the reading, has to be the one typing in the booking (or calling you, depending on how you handle bookings). I promise you that this advice will save you a lot of headaches. Clients need to know what they are getting into and have the time to back out if it doesn't feel right. Perhaps a husband has lost his father and is grieving in silence, and his wife (your former client) wants to give him a reading to connect with his father and work through his grief. It's a very loving and caring gesture from the wife, but the husband may not be ready for a reading. You can end up sitting with a client who doesn't want to be there. So, no surprise bookings.

Coaching-type readings

Some readings have a bit of a coaching type of feel, and these readings are usually a little more of the psychic type. This is no problem if you keep working on your clairs and give them that type of evidence or information. But, if you feel that you have life experience connected to the client's problem and start providing them with advice, you lose the reading. There's nothing to say that your solution to the same problem is the right solution for the client—it may be the opposite. If you, at any point, feel the urge to give some personal advice, then just say, "This is from me, not from my mediumship."

Doing vs. talking

When you do mediumship, don't *talk* about mediumship. There will come a day when you feel confident and experienced enough to teach others how to do this. But on your way there, stick to the evidence. I'm saying this because you will undergo many changes in your mediumship. Over time, you may feel that your first point of view wasn't correct. Then, later on in your journey, you may feel you have a complete picture of this subject and are ready to teach. So there is no point in starting to teach before you are prepared. I usually say when you have answered the same questions a thousand times with identical answers, you will know your truth about mediumship is pretty stabilized. An important note here: your way of teaching this, one day in the future, may be completely different from my way of teaching this here. That's okay, that's how mediumship evolves. There are many ways of doing and teaching this subject.

Bad connection

If you can't get a connection to the spirit, stop the reading and don't charge your client. If you have tried for forty-eight minutes of a fifty-minute reading and still feel unsatisfied, the client doesn't have to pay for it. If the client is super satisfied, but you feel that you messed up, or didn't do your best, then the client doesn't have to pay for it. If the client, for any reason, is dissatisfied even if you just gave them the best reading of your life, then they don't have to pay for it. This may sound strange to some. Why shouldn't you get paid for your time? Well, see this as a piece of business advice. If you are honest in your work and set expectations on yourself to always do your best, this will grow your business very fast. If you get into arguments, take money from dissatisfied customers, or always claim that you're right, you will end your own business in a heartbeat. (In the bonus section of this course, we will talk more about the business side of mediumship.) Remember to be professional, "If you burn the fries, don't charge for the burger." People *need* to go to the dentist but they don't *need* to go to a medium—they do it because they want to. And if people don't get a pleasant and professional experience, neither they nor their friends will come back. As the world looks right now, mediumship is, for many people, still seen as entertainment. If we can't get them in the door and show them that mediumship is so much more, we will have fewer opportunities to do this thing that we love.

Responsible for their own lives

And finally, remember: every person is responsible for their own life. No matter how hard or unfair our lives have been, we are still responsible for how we choose to handle it. Your job as a medium is not to save people, it's to give evidence. And even if a client says their whole life or happiness is in your hands, they are wrong. Be a medium with an open office for anyone to book a reading, don't work in a closed bubble reading the same ten people repeatedly. Working with new people and clients will have a positive ripple-effect on your business. Only do readings that are pre-booked according to your chosen schedule and say no to everything after hours. Don't be someone's personal medium, always available on the phone and answering questions in the middle of the night, getting all involved in someone's life. Be professional! No matter how big or small your mediumship business is, it should always be a business. You are you; you are not your business.

These are some important points I want you to keep in the back of your mind. Outside these points, there are many other important ones, but most fit under the umbrella of common sense. If something feels wrong, it usually is, and once you get some continuity in your readings, all of this will feel like second nature.

Step 9: Groups & Demonstrations

In this step, we will talk about working with groups and doing demonstrations of mediumship. I know this type of work may be a bit in the future and not something you want to get going with right away, which is understandable. The reason I want to talk about this is once you get your mediumship going and start doing more readings and have more satisfied customers, this question will arise: "Can you do a reading for me and my friends?" This question will probably come sooner than you think.

Group readings

Of course, a "group reading" is a reading for a group of usually between five to fifteen people. A group reading is a normal reading. You do it the same way, but you try to connect to a couple more spirit contacts, and if possible, try to jump from one person to the next. The word "group" may, for some beginning mediums, feel a bit scary. That's because when we think of working with a group, we can lose the right focus and start thinking about our performance instead. But think back to the example I did with the man in the hospital wanting you to deliver a message to his son. A group reading is the same, it's not about you, you are only the telephone, the link to the other side. People or clients in a group reading are usually much more relaxed; working with groups is one of the best and nicest settings in which to do mediumship.

More spirits will be waiting on the other side when there are more people in the room. In the beginning stages of working with groups, it's normal not to know who the spirit contact is connected to. But keep the questions in mind as you work and deliver the evidence through your clairs. After a couple of pieces of good evidence, ask the group, "Does anyone recognize this?" If your description is too vague, several people will recognize what you are saying. If you continue to ask the other side your silent questions, you will gain more specific evidence, and then only one person will recognize what you are saying. Then, you just keep working with that person the same as you do in a private reading. If there are fifteen people and your group reading is scheduled for, let's say, one hour, then you have to work a little faster. No psychic stuff, just contact, evidence, message, and move on. Sometimes you may feel that more than one spirit wants to come through, if this happens, just pick one and take the others later. Some experienced mediums can acknowledge multiple spirits: "I have a man here with a heart condition, a woman who loved horses, and a young man in a motorcycle accident." After acknowledging them, they work with one spirit at a time. They present multiple spirit contacts to keep the group engaged, so they will know that their loved one is coming even if someone has to wait till the end of the reading. For me, this splits my energy a little, so I like to bring through one at a time and have the other spirits queue on the other side.

Mediumship demonstrations

Then we have "demonstrations," which are the same as groups but with a larger audience. A demonstration can be anything from twenty to a hundred people, but for me, a normal-sized demonstration is about fifty to seventy (and, of course, some celebrity mediums do venues with a thousand people). The difference with demonstrations, especially in the beginning, is that these are usually something you get invited to do. It can be a spiritual center, a bookstore, or something similar, and there will be an organizer in charge of everything—you just need to show up.

I want to tell you a short story about the first real demonstration I ever did. The organizer had sold fifty tickets. The room was going to be filled, and they booked me to do a ninety-minute demonstration. They usually give you a separate room to prepare in so you don't have to see or be disturbed by the audience as they arrive at the venue. At this specific venue, they had the preparation room on stage, like a small closet just to the side of it. So, I could walk in from one side, and then when it was show time, I could just open a door and be right on the stage. I arrived forty-five minutes before I was scheduled to start, and I sat in this room meditating. But the walls were so thin that I could hear the people filling the room. I couldn't hear what they said, but I could hear this buzzing sound of people coming in through the doors. And, of course, being my first demonstration, I lost focus for a moment and started to get nervous. As I listened to my meditation music, I could hear my heart pounding faster. I could feel my pulse hitting hard. And for about twenty minutes, I had to wrestle with this before everything went silent. I walked on-stage, probably mumbling some introduction, and then I started. And the exciting thing was, and this has been one of the best learning moments in my career, that even though my body was very nervous, my mind, my mediumistic connection, was unaffected. My mediumship worked fine, and after a while, I relaxed. It was a fantastic experience.

With the knowledge the other side is helping you and doing their part of the equation, you can relax and let go of the performance aspect of your demonstration. You will have good demonstrations and bad demonstrations. It is what it is. Own the experience and use it to develop as a medium and person. When you show the spirit world that you are ready to step up, take on the challenge and do your best. They will come and help you get the job done. It may take a while before you are ready to work with groups or do demonstrations. Commonly, mediums just starting out with demonstrations do it with others, maybe two or three mediums simultaneously. They take turns and do one or two contacts each. This is good because it lets a little of the pressure go, and in the beginning, it can also be a little too energy-consuming to hold connections for ninety minutes.

I hope I have inspired you to keep this whole group and demonstration thing as an exciting step in the future. Everything you practice, you will get better at. And I know that, just as all people can develop mediumship, so too can all people take it to the stage.

Step 10: What Happens Next?

So, here we are! This is the last step in the course, and even though there is an important bonus section left, this is the final step on the development ladder we have been climbing throughout the course. Before you go to the bonus section, I want you to have finished the exercise sheet and ticked off all the boxes. To get the most out of the bonus section, its good to have the experience from the different exercises.

Is this the end?

What now? Is this the end of your mediumistic journey? Of course not, now the fun begins! We have gone through this process and created a theoretical and mental concept of the art of mediumship. We have done the exercises to gain experience, and by now you understand that we can think and believe a lot of stuff about this subject, but once we feel it, once we understand the clairs and how communication works, we know the reality of it. We are no longer just mentally interested in mediumship. Now, we are mediums working on our actual skills.

From this point onwards, there will still be a lot of questions popping up, and you will still drift back and forth in your confidence when it comes to mediumship and readings. I can tell you that even very experienced mediums question this whole thing from time to time. The way we keep it real and alive is by helping our clients. Each time you bring a spirit contact through for a client, you see the significance in your work. You will have good and bad days but my mantra has always been that "the bad days are the days I develop the most," because that's what it's all about, continuous development. The journey of mediumship development never ends, and you get better each time you do it. I sometimes look back at my first readings and think: "I wonder why some clients didn't just stand up and walk out?" Well, of course they didn't. I did my absolute best with the right intentions, and the spirit world helped me and gave me what I needed. Ten years from now, I may look back at this course and think, why didn't I say it like *this* or explain it like *that*. We do our best in the moment, with the right intentions, and then we move on. Some will say that you are a fantastic medium, and others will say you are not a medium at all. It doesn't matter; it is what it is.

The important thing is never to let it stop you. One day you will have twenty years of experience in this, and then you will understand that everything that happened along the way was part of your development and had nothing but a positive effect.

When you finish this course, you won't be alone. This book will still be here, and hopefully, you have connected to some like-minded friends through the exercises. But from now on, I want you to see yourself as a medium, not a student. You can still be a student when you do the exercises within this book, but start looking for "real" clients. Work with a professional approach. I go on about this "being professional" thing because students sometimes tend to pull the brakes a little when it's time to do something real. I want you to do this totally for real and approach every client, group, or demonstration as though you have done it thousands of times. Come back to this course if you have questions, thoughts, or there's something you don't understand. Find your answers, and go back out and work again.

In the bonus section

In the first bonus section, I will talk a little more about the business side of mediumship. I have already mentioned I always see the calling of mediumship as a job. Being a medium and regularly doing readings should be seen as a business. However, I don't say "business" from an economic perspective (even though you are allowed to make money through your mediumship). I say business from a structural perspective. If you do your mediumship and see it as a business (even if you only do three readings a month), you allow yourself to only work when you're working. People will respect your structure, and over time this can become a part- or full-time job, if you like, because the structure is already there. If you have no structure, you could end up being on the telephone in the middle of the night doing pro bono readings for desperate people who need other help.

Doing mediumship takes energy, and I'm not only talking about spiritual energy, I mean normal physical energy. Just as you can't do any other job twenty-four hours a day, it's the same with mediumship. And just as you go on vacation from a regular job, you also need a break from mediumship. I recommend at least eight to ten weeks of break from mediumship each year. You can still meditate during this period if you want, but no readings. And after a break like this, you will find that your connection and mediumship have grown stronger. When I did my first group reading for Warner Brothers, the company that produces the TV show, I hadn't done a signal link or connection for three months before walking into that meeting. I knew that if it were meant to be, the spirit world would help me, and they did, big time.

The one-year workout plan

So, to keep this development ball rolling, I have created a one-year workout plan, which you can find at the end of this step. This workout plan is structured like the exercise sheet, with the purpose of pushing yourself a little and keeping the momentum going. During this year, you should keep returning to this course and see how the information on these pages starts to gain a deeper meaning in your work. As you will see in this one-year workout plan, much of it is based on mediumistic readings and step seven of this course. So, now and then, I want you to go back to this section and repeat the material because it represents how you should work as you move forward with your mediumship. Try to do at least some reading every week and, if possible, find some daily activity connected to your development. Do the meditation exercise and read books by other mediums—I recommend Scottish medium Gordon Smith. One thing we also talked about in the divination section is having a deck of cards on your coffee table to play around with when you have some spare time, just to stimulate the clairs.

Welcome to your future

Okay, this is not a goodbye, but a welcome to the next level on your development journey. From this point, anything is possible, and you are now free to choose how you wish to sculpt the future of your mediumship, to tweak and develop your style in any way you want to, and you are always welcome to come back to this book if you need inspiration or answers. In the upcoming years, mediumship will change. Not only your mediumship, but the worldview on this subject. Fewer people will see this subject with a "yes" or "no" attitude, and more people will be interested in exploring the possibilities of this sixth sense. You are entering the world of mediumship at a very interesting and exciting time. Not long from now, the services we provide will become essential to many people. So, keep moving forward. Step into your professional shoes, do the best you can, and take every opportunity that comes your way. We can always do much more than we think, and we never get challenges we can't handle. When things start to feel too comfortable, it's time for the next step, so bring on new challenges. Keep your momentum, be a professional medium with the right focus and a playful mind, and you will do great.

Thank you!

It has been an absolute pleasure and honor to do this course with you. I have done my best to make all the steps as good and effective as possible with the intention of giving you a fun, fast, and easy way to explore your skills and develop your mediumship. For me, this course represents a modern way of development, and I hope you have enjoyed it as much as I have.

I look forward to seeing and hearing about your work, and I hope your name will pop up in the future as someone recognized in the field of mediumship. So, thank you so much!

One-Year Workout Plan

Step 2 | Exercise 1 | Expanding in Stillness | 20 minutes.

(Do this exercise as often as you can, minimum 4 days a week)

Step 4 | Exercise 3 | Psychic Reading | 20 x 20 minutes

Step 6 | Exercise 4 | Divination | 20 x 20 minutes

Step 7 | Exercise 6 | Mediumship | 30 x 30 minutes

<u>Activity Calendar</u>, mark how many weeks of the year you have been active and done any of the exercises on this One-Year Workout Plan.

Bonus Section

Five secrets to successful spiritual business

Welcome to the bonus section! As discussed in the course, I see mediumship as a business for several reasons. First, it doesn't matter if you do it as a hobby or a full-time business, there still has to be some structure to what you do if you want to have the time and money to keep doing it. I never saw mediumship as a potential income source, and I spent about $40,000 over twelve years doing courses and workshops in Sweden and other countries. I bought all the books, tapes, and lectures, went to demonstrations and book signings, and went to endless mediums for readings to see how they worked and their different styles. Having spent a lot of time and money on development, I have recognized two things. To continue to develop your skills, you need to spend time on them, and to be able to do that, you also need to have the funds. It doesn't matter if it's just a hobby, you are still providing a service to other people, and a pretty unique one, too. So, your clients should pay you for your time.

If you structure your services as a business, no matter how small it may be, you are automatically opening the doors for more business. If you have an open office where anyone can book a reading, they will. So we will go through five factors that will help you get clients to ensure you can keep the momentum in your mediumship and afford to keep doing it. If you, like me, have young children, motivating yourself to go away for a couple of days working and not getting paid is hard because you have to make up for that time and loss of income with other work—it becomes an endless cycle. If you get paid, you can relax, know your family's well-being is secured, and spend time with them without having to take on multiple jobs. And I know that not everybody wants to do this full-time, but the same example still applies no matter how much you do it.

So, the five secrets, are five things that tend to get overlooked when spiritually-minded people get into business. Not all spiritual people as per se, but many of them.

Secret #1: Right brain, left brain

Have you ever seen the show X-Factor, with all those amazing singers who have spent their whole lives trying, but never got near the door of a record company even though seemingly less-talented singers are on the radio every day? Talking about personality types again, what I'm saying is that some spiritually-minded people tend to think: "If I stay in my spiritual bubble, the universe will provide." I'm sorry, but we live in a physical world, and the laws of this world still apply even if you are a spiritual person. This is why I'm trying to be as clear as possible about changing frequency, going to the right places, coming back out, and getting on with your life. There is no point in being a "lightworker" or a medium if you are going to be broke, depleted of energy, overworked, and feeling sick and tired all the time. The truth is that you won't attract any clients if you don't have a functional work structure. I hope you can follow me here: sometimes you meet very spiritual and nice people, but they feel a bit delusional for some reason. They talk like everything is perfect, love and light, but their energy and aura sends a completely different message. This happens because some people can't handle the circumstances or feelings of their life, so they go into the spiritual bubble to hide and never come out. There's nothing wrong with this, it's freedom of choice, and it is what it is. But I'm saying that to be a good medium, you also need a normal stable life here on earth. People who walk around telling everybody to "ground yourself" or using phrases like "that's just your ego" are only reflecting something within themselves.

You want to figure out how much mediumship you want to do, structure your time, and set your own rules for your business. If some of your clients don't accept these rules, then they are the wrong clients for you. Think left brain, right brain; do mediumship with the right and business with the left.

Secret #2: Abundance of clients

At the beginning of your mediumship career, you may feel lonely and question yourself. Am I on the right path? No one seems interested in booking a reading with me. . . . But I promise you, keep going, the clients will come. There are more clients worldwide (and in your own town) than you could possibly imagine. But the thing about mediumship is that clients usually want to check you out for a while before the book. They need to go back to your website several times, maybe read your Facebook posts, and basically get a sense of you for a while. Then suddenly, out of nowhere, you find yourself fully booked. The clients are out there, and your specific clients will be perfect for you because they are drawn to you as a person. It doesn't matter if you have a super famous TV medium living next door; your clients will come to you. For five years, I had a place in a part of Stockholm, Sweden, called the "old town." This is not a big place, but I think we were at least ten mediums working there, most of us full-time and fully booked. But sometimes, it takes a little while before these things happen, and this is, unfortunately, the moment when many beginning mediums pull the brakes. They stop doing mediumship only to realize a year or two later that they wish they hadn't quit, and at that moment, they try to get it going again. Just keep your calendar open for business, and the clients will come.

Secret #3: Focus your business

I'm not talking about focusing *on* your business, I'm talking about "focusing your business." What do I mean? Who do you call if you want to order a great pizza? Who do you call if your toilet is clogged up? Would you like if both of these services were on the same phone number? NO! You don't want the plumber to make your pizza. Although nothing says that the plumber *couldn't* make you a fantastic pizza, it just feels wrong. We like to hire an expert for every specific service. We don't like when they mix too much. And this is a problem I always see in the field of mediumship and spiritual business. Sometimes people are not confident enough in their mediumship, so they add a resume to their mediumship title to make them look more qualified, but it has the opposite effect. "Medium, healer, and certified business coach," "medium, regression therapist, and life coach," "medium, lawyer, and 5th-dimensional chakra balancer." I hope you see what I mean here. It doesn't matter if you are an accountant, a mechanic, or a mother of five, this information only shatters the focus of your business, and your clients start to think: "Hmm. . . . If that person went to law school, they couldn't have had much time to develop and perfect their skills as a medium." If, for example, you quit your job and open a coffee shop, then you become interested in building boats, and finally you start developing mediumship, you will then have three things, or businesses, going on, and together they could become your full-time job. Fantastic, that's great! You are doing what you like. But you don't put all of these on the same business card, and you don't casually throw in: "So, you want to order a boat? Great! Did I tell you I'm also a medium?" NO . . . you don't.

The focus here is to keep your service as clear and precise as possible. Personally, I have had a lot of training in the field of healing, and I hold multiple certificates from pretty extensive healing training. But I don't write "medium and healer" on my website, even if these two services are very closely related. For me, I see it as two different jobs. I know how much time, training, and effort goes into both of them, and I would not go to a medium for healing—I would go to a specialized healer. You are, of course, absolutely welcome to try this out yourself, but when it comes to mediumship, I know that potential clients are very sensitive to mixing different services. If you just call yourself a medium and then your name, e.g., Medium Marie, you will be booked for many more readings.

Secret #4: Pricing

If you have lower prices, you will get more customers, right? No. What would you think if you walked by a hair salon and the sign said: "Haircut $2"? You would probably think about lack of quality. The same goes for readings. If you price it too low, no one, or maybe one or two weird ones, will book you. If you price it a little higher, a few more will come, but they will be dissatisfied no matter how good your reading is. If clients don't pay enough for a reading, they have a tendency to simply not believe what you say. But with the right professional price, you will have their attention *and* their manners because they will take you seriously. I'm not talking about tricking people with your price. I'm talking about you getting paid like every other person or service out there.

I have always been interested in human potential. About nine years ago, I studied NLP coaching parallel to working as a medium, and I am now what's called a master practitioner of NLP. If I did a website today, marketing myself as a coach, I could probably charge double or triple the price per hour I do as a medium. Many who work in the spiritual field have somehow bought into the belief that we shouldn't charge for our time like everyone else. I used to get emails from people saying, "Do you charge for your readings? I didn't think that was allowed." By who, the spirit world? Try to walk into the supermarket and say, "I shouldn't have to pay for this food, I'm a medium, and I work for free." They will have security escort you out. We are incarnated in these bodies and have to live by the same life rules and charge for our time just like everyone else. And this is what you do to make it work.

You charge full price, or at least a good price, from the beginning. In my opinion, once you get going, your rate should start at a minimum of about $70–80 and pretty soon go up to $100 (these are Swedish prices, 2022). I know that the market and costs for readings are very different in different countries, and that £70 for a reading in England, for example, is pretty high. So, you should think like this: what is the average price for a known and established medium in your area? Don't compare yourself with services such as massage therapy, beauty therapists, or any other service that can build up a list of regular customers. They can also hand their work over to a colleague if they go on vacation. You don't have that luxury. You have to see yourself as a consultant delivering a unique service that no one else can do, and over time, you can charge $200 if you want to. Think like this: I charge full price, but if the reading doesn't work, they get it for free—no discounts or holiday sales. You set a reasonable price from the beginning, and then if two out of six readings don't work on a particular day, you still have gotten paid sufficiently for at least four hours of your work. I know that for some starting mediums, its sometimes hard to accept this strategy. They want to start small and cheap, but you need to get over it. One of the biggest mistakes you can make is starting at a really low price and then trying to raise it later, your clients won't accept that. If you raise your prices from $75 to $80 at the beginning of the year, that's no problem, but if you jump from $20 to $100, you will lose all your business for a long time. People see your price, accept it, and then book. Your price will find the right clients. Some people need at least a $100 price point, any lower than that and they feel the quality isn't good enough. I know mediums charging $300–$500 for an hour of reading, and they are fully booked.

Secret #5: The humble approach

This is a simple but very profound secret. Whatever happens in your readings, your interactions with clients, groups, or other mediums, always let go of the urge to be right. You will meet people who try to push your buttons, either saying you're mistaken, or you're doing it wrong, or that I have taught you something wrong. This is all mental drama, and it can only affect you if you let it. I have colleagues in this business who constantly deal with difficult clients, don't always get along with someone, and are always questioned about their work. They are great mediums, but there is far too much baggage and drama connected to their work. If you cultivate the habit of letting things go, it won't stick to you. If a client wants to take you for a spin and give you a hard time, just say, "Sorry, I can't get a good link for you." Blame it on yourself and let them go. They want nothing more than to start an argument. Just send them home immediately, don't charge them anything, and move on.

Once you get going and are recognized as a professional medium, the world of mediumship can feel everything but spiritual. Some people do mediumship to help others, while others do it for recognition. The ones that do it for recognition don't want to have you stealing their thunder. I may be painting a dismal picture here, but you can be free from all of this. Stay away from the drama and focus on your work as a medium. Let your mediumship guide you on where to go next, and let your work create all the opportunities you deserve to develop and get your message out to the world. This is not just a key secret to mediumship, it's a key secret to life. No one can stop you if you walk your unique path through life. There will be many people on the way telling you to turn left or right, but just keep going. The universe has got a unique plan just for you.

Five great tips

In this section, I will tell you five of the best tips and tricks that I have developed over the years to elevate a *good* reading to an *excellent* one. These are just small things I do to distract my brain, shift my focus, get to the right place, and connect to the spirit world as fast as possible. I have purposefully put these in the back of the book because I wanted you to gain experience from the exercises before trying these.

Tip #1: Feel the client from the first second

If you have prepared yourself properly, you can start to feel the client before they even enter the door. As you open the door and let them in, feel them (not physically, of course, feel them through your clairs). I'm not talking about "cold reading" or "reading body language" here. I'm talking about energy. If you, for example, have a female client coming through the door, feel her energy. As you feel her energy, you will start to understand who she is through your clairs and get an intial picture or feeling of her family. There is a big chance she has many of her parents' personality traits. So, by feeling your client's energy, you also feel her mother or father. If, for example, her mother is in the spirit world, you can use that feeling to get your first connection: the mother. This may sound very complicated, but it's absolutely not. Try it. Just be aware of your clairs as the client walks in through the door, and you will feel the spirits coming in with her.

Tip #2: The muscle relaxer

If you, for any reason, are struggling to get a connection to the spirit, stop, take a deep breath and imagine that everything inside your body is being flushed out as you release the breath. Breathe in, empty your body through your feet as you breathe out, and just sit with that feeling for three seconds. Suddenly your clairs will then throw something into this feeling, and you will put your focus there and build on that information. Don't show your client that you are doing this, just do it. Empty, and quickly catch the first thing that comes: milk, dog, umbrella, etc. The information is always there, and your clairs will help you get the connection you need.

Tip #3: Provoke an emotion

If you are having a hard time getting the reading going or your client's energy feels a little closed-off, look them right in the eyes and keep looking. This behavior can seem a little awkward, and the client may get a little uncomfortable for a second, but there you have it. Right in that moment of discomfort, the client will shift their energy. And by doing so, they also use energy, and their energy field, or aura, will suddenly get stronger. Now you can catch that energy, connect with them, and follow that energy to the spirit world. This may also sound complicated, but it's not. Look in their eyes without blinking, and you will see the energy and the reading start to flow.

Tip #4: The water trick

If you feel you are connecting with your client, but the information is a little vague and you can't quite grasp the evidence, or you are just slightly wrong in everything you say. Then stop, take a breath, and reach for the glass of water (by the way, you and your client should always have a glass of fresh water close by). So, take the glass, look down into the water (don't make this too obvious to the client), and just relax like there's no client in the room. Now, you can use the water in the glass as a divination tool, let it give you some psychic information about your client, then build on that information.

Tip #5: Look at their hands

This is also a powerful divination tool. Look at the client's hands and imagine what these hands would look like if they were older. You don't need to hold their hands, just look at them silently from a distance and see them grow older. When the hands look old enough, try to picture the person connected to these hands, and there you have it, your next spirit contact.

These are the five tricks I use almost every day in my work. Some may seem too simple while others too complicated, but I promise you, these are all very easy things you can learn and use, and you will soon realize how powerful and effective they are.

Recording your readings

Before we finish this book, there is just one more thing I want to talk about. Something I spoke briefly about during the course was recording your readings. I have always used a voice recorder during my readings, which has always been included in the price. Using the recorder is a way to give yourself a little insurance if you start it before your introduction, as no one can say they didn't know what they were getting into.

But, the most important thing with the voice recorder has always been that I use it as a quality stamp for myself.

Whenever you record a reading, at some point it will likely be played back to family or friends, and it becomes your best business card ever. But if you feel you don't want anyone to listen to the recording because you haven't delivered as a medium after a reading, just say: "Sorry, but I'm not satisfied with this reading. I offer this: you keep your money, I keep the recording, and if you want to, you are welcome back at another time or you can use your money to see another medium. It's important for me you get a good reading. I don't feel I did that for you today." This may sound strange.

However, if you use the recording as a quality meter for yourself, in your work, you will come across as very professional, can always charge a reasonable price, and know that friends and family of the client are hearing an excellent recording. The client you just had will likely come back, making it a win-win. Don't charge for it if you are unsatisfied with what you just did. This attitude will give you many more clients and business in the long run.

Our Own Loved Ones

Many people starting this journey towards mediumship do it for a specific reason. Over the years, there is one question I have answered more than any other: "If I develop mediumship, will I be able to communicate with my own loved ones in the spirit world?" I absolutely understand the longing underneath this question, and it's also how I, many years ago, ended up on this path. But the truth is that our memories, pictures, and love for those we have lost often overpower our spiritual senses. It gets hard to separate ourselves from spirit communication and we end up with too many white marbles.

To develop one's skills and use them to help others is a beautiful thing, something you can always be proud of. But unfortunately, most of us will always be too close to our own feelings to get a clean link to our family on the other side. So, what we do as mediums, when we need the same services we provide to others, is simply to book a reading. We release the urge to do it on our own and treat ourselves to a reading by another medium. Then we can love, laugh, and cry the same way our own clients do, knowing that the ones we have lost are always right there, by our side.

About the Author

Johan Poulsen is an acclaimed psychic medium, author, lecturer, and teacher. Born in Stockholm, Sweden, Johan's fascination with the spirit world began at a young age. He dedicated much of his time to learning all he could about the mysteries of the spirit world. For the past thirteen years, Johan has worked to share his knowledge and educate others about mediumship and psychic abilities. He helps people change their beliefs and embrace their innate abilities through public appearances, television, and his writing.

Known for his straightforward, no-nonsense approach, Johan has done thousands of private readings, taught mediumship to over a thousand students, participated in interviews, given stage demonstrations, contributed to various magazines, and starred in the Warner Bros. show *Swedish Mediums*. Johan lives in the south of Sweden with his family.

www.developmediumship.com

Made in United States
North Haven, CT
20 March 2024

50205794R00114